41

DEPOSITS

41

DEPOSITS

Crucial
Conversations
for
Fathers
and Sons

STEVE GRAVES

B&H
PUBLISHING
NASHVILLE, TENNESSEE

Published by B&H Publishing Group
Nashville, Tennessee

Dewey Decimal Classification: 306.874
Subject Heading: FATHER-SON RELATIONSHIP /
FATHERS / SONS / CHRISTIAN LIFE

Cover design by Faceout Studio; Lindy Martin.
Texture images © HorenkO and Roobcio /
Shutterstock. Son image © andreas-dress-769662-unsplash.
Dad image © natalie-toombs-450149-unsplash.

1 2 3 4 5 6 • 23 22 21 20 19

To my son, Kile, and the God we both follow. And to every parent trying to prepare and launch their kids into the world with love, sound footing, and confidence.

Acknowledgments

I crafted the ideas and packaged them into the chapters in this book, but every chapter and each core message have roots that span into someone who strategically influenced me. In other words, I am simply passing along deposits others have made in me along my journey.

My mom has fingerprints on more chapters than she will ever know. My wife helped me figure out how to parent in a real-world setting. My girls, Katelyn and Julianne, gave me grace in the times when I failed with them first so as to recover and do better with Kile. Friends, colleagues, and mentors have fine-tuned and edited my theories and theology throughout my life. Thanks to you all.

A special shout-out to Chris Ferebee, my agent. I am certain I am the most frustrating and least productive author he represents. Thanks for the decades of friendship.

And, I was honored to have Stephen Caldwell, former colleague on *The Life@Work Journal*, bring his extraordinary skill-set to the project. Additionally, the publishing team at LifeWay has made this project even more meaningful for me. Thanks to you all.

Last, I wake up each day astounded that God still loves and pursues me. The Lord has been my "dad" my entire life. He has been the father guiding and loving me each step of my life. I hope this project ties a tighter knot between you and your Creator, as well as between you and your children.

Contents

Introduction:
Heart-Knot Deposits

*A strong gift can take you where the absences
of other gifts cannot keep you.*

—Anonymous

A friend and I were wade fishing on the Buffalo National River in northern Arkansas when a feeling of dread came over us. It was a fabulous spring day in the Ozarks. The sun was shining. The flowers and trees were in bloom. The birds were talking and the fish were biting. Then, while casting our lines as we stood knee-deep in the cool, clear water, we noticed something from the corners of our eyes—our boat was floating away from the bank!

We were in the middle of nowhere, literally miles from the nearest town, home, or campground. This was the remote bottom twenty-three miles that flows into the White River with no access. We had a problem without our boat. So, we threw down our rods and chased the boat—for the rest of the day. Instead of hauling in small mouth bass, we climbed steep banks, ran around trees, and jumped over rocks in pursuit of our ride back to civilization.

We had tied our boat to a tree stump, but the knot was weak and the rope eventually slipped loose. The current turned the boat into a floating version of Usain Bolt—always just a bit faster than its competition. Every time I rounded a corner, I saw the boat slip out of sight around the next bend in the river. Reconnecting with it became a long and arduous ordeal, and it cost us time, energy, and (we like to think) quite a few fish.

I've come to believe that it's each parent's calling to tie a knot between his or her heart and the heart of their children through every season of life. The prophet Malachi pictured a day when the Lord would "turn the heart of fathers to their children and the hearts of children to their fathers" (Mal. 4:6). But the currents in the river of life work against these "heart-knots," and from time to time they can unravel. Parents can mistakenly think they only need to tie one really tight knot when their children are young and then sit back and hope it doesn't unravel. People are human—we do stupid things. Relationships are difficult, even with those we love. Growth and change happen—think puberty, graduation, adulthood—and life is hard. Circumstances often are beyond our control. But the greater the integrity of the heart-knot, the less likely it will slip loose and allow the relationship to drift away. So, we should never pass on opportunities to invest in the integrity of the heart-knot with those we love.

When our son, Kile, entered high school, I decided to make an intentional, long-term investment into our heart-knot. Frankly, it's something I regret not doing with more intent with our two older daughters, but I didn't want to make the same mistake a third time around. So, in the fall of his sophomore year, Kile and I began going to a new bagel shop to discuss life over breakfast. Over the next three years, we talked about each of the "deposits" you'll find in this book.

I'm not sure of the precise moment I decided to launch these discussions, but I can trace it back at least in part to a twentieth anniversary vacation with my wife in Italy. Karen and I were in Venice when we noticed a small, mom-and-pop leather shop during our daily walk through a neighborhood across the canal from our hotel. We stopped in each morning, browsed through the merchandise, and visited with the sociable young man who was taking over the family business. It only took a few days for him to seem like a lifelong friend. And on our last day in town, I made a purchase: three high-quality, leather-bound journals, one for each of our children.

Since Kile was about to begin high school, I decided I would fill his journal with fatherly advice and give it to him a few years later as a graduation present. The more I thought about it, however, the more I realized there was an opportunity for something more—a chance for me to give Kile something I'd never gotten from my father. I would not just give him practical wisdom, but structured time together during a season of life we would never be able to relive.

The idea behind the journal morphed into the regular discussions between Kile and me at the bagel shop. We didn't meet on a formal schedule but as our calendars allowed. I drove the agenda and the timing, ensuring that we met at least a couple of times each month and that the discussions had purpose. But we were light on structure and formalities. Sometimes we spent several weeks on the same deposit. Sometimes we covered it over one bagel. And sometimes we ditched the planned conversation in favor of some challenge or issue that had sprung up in his life or mine.

Spending time with Kile to discuss those deposits helped create integrity in our heart-knot because it provided a platform for building strength into our relationship—it allowed us to discuss important issues, for him to honor my role as his father, for me to respect his growth as a budding man, and for us to set the foundation for conversations we now have as adults.

Addressing the real-time opportunities was critical to the integrity of our heart-knot. I wanted Kile to know the relationship was far more important than my preplanned agenda. At the same time, it was important that we also cover some very specific topics. I wanted to make two types of deposits in his life—relational deposits and wisdom deposits—and, for me, both were highly personal and equally important.

This all might sound a bit odd. *Deposit* is a financial term, right? When we deposit money in a bank, it's primarily a business transaction. It's not personal, certainly not to the bank (no matter how much the bank might claim to love us in its ads). When we make deposits into someone we love, however, that's a different story. Relational deposits are personal. So, I'm using that term in a very personal, very relational way.

The other important thing to remember about deposits is that they often require time to reap rewards, and, in fact, there are no guarantees that any rewards at all will result.

With Kile, my goal was pretty simple: to make wisdom deposits into his mind and relational deposits into his heart. I wasn't trying to get an immediate transformation, nor was I trying to check some box to make me feel better about myself. There was no test he had to pass, and I didn't expect him to agree with me or automatically adopt my way of thinking. Instead, I expected him to listen and share his thoughts and feelings enough that I could see in his eyes or hear in his words something that served as a receipt acknowledging the deposit had been made.

The importance of these discussions, by the way, also was personal to me, because I didn't get these types of deposits, wisdom or relational, from my father.

I often tell people I defied the odds.

In 1960, 89 percent of the children in the United States lived in homes where their fathers were present. Among the other 11 percent was a toddler of a mostly single mom who was making her way in the Gulf Coast region. That toddler was me.

The percentage of children without a father in their home has risen steadily over the years, and now it's estimated that one of three kids in the United States—some 24 million children—fit in that category.[1] The challenges for these kids are serious. Compared to children with their fathers in the home, they are more likely to live in poverty, to have behavioral problems, to abuse drugs and alcohol, to suffer from obesity, to drop out of high school, to commit a crime, and to go to prison. And the girls are seven times more likely to become pregnant before they turn twenty.[2]

You can see why I tell people I defied the odds.

How did I do it? I would begin, of course, with crediting the grace of God. But God works through His people, and He worked through several people who invested in my life. Certainly, I had to do my part, but I find it hard to imagine how my life would have turned out without the deposits of people like Mr. Cherry (a neighbor mentor when I was a child), Coach Rogers (my basketball coach), Pastor Baker (a pastor in college), Dr. Shields (my favorite college professor), Manley Beasley (a minister and mentor), and, of course, my mother (GeGe, as she is affectionately known among family and friends).

Throughout the most formative years of my life journey, those people saw something in me worthy of their investment, and so they made a series of deposits that paid off—for me, if not for them—many times over.

While I am proof that a kid without the steering hand of a biological father in his life still can succeed, I am also very aware that the mere physical presence of a father in a home is no guarantee that the children will turn out great. Even the presence of the best father is no guarantee. But the odds absolutely improve for children who have an active, engaged, loving father who is making deposits into their lives, working hard to tie a sturdy heart-knot. Thus, much of my energy to be a good parent was fueled by a desire to give my three children something I'd never gotten from my biological father but that I thankfully had gotten from others.

The more you experience life as a parent, I've decided, the more you realize there is nothing you can mess up so badly that God can't redeem for your children, and nothing you do well eliminates your children's obligation to make their own choices and reap their own results. As a parent, I have regrets. I missed some opportunities and failed at others. But I also did a few things well along the way, and I believe my regular heart-knot meetings with Kile are among those things.

No Silver Bullets

The idea of putting these deposits together into a book came with some mixed emotions.

At the risk of having you stop reading before you even finish the first chapter, here's the reality: I didn't come up with these deposits for you or your son—I came up with them for Kile. And while I edited these deposits for the book to give them some flow and consistency, they remain, at their essence, a collection of discussion points that are mostly about my experience with my son rather than universal prescriptions for success in parenting or life.

This isn't a book about how I'm the perfect dad with perfect kids who is going to tell you how I did it so that if you'll just do what I did, then you'll end up with perfect kids, too. We live in a prescriptive world, but I have a strong bias against silver-bullet prescriptions for life. Even in my CEO coaching practice I hate silver bullet solutions. So, this isn't a self-help book. It's more of a help-yourself book. These deposits reflect the context of our personal journey, not the be-all, end-all advice for every father in the world.

On the other hand, there is value in collective wisdom. We all learn from one another. None of these deposits reflect bad advice (I hope!), and I believe they all provide guiding truths that will serve any father and son well.

I also waivered on whether to write this book because the last thing I want is for Kile to feel any additional pressure to live his journey out in front of others with this as a backdrop. Some deposits were covered because he struggled in a particular area at that time, but many were simply universal truths I wanted to make sure he knew. And, by the way, we ended up with forty-one because that's how the timing worked out. I originally planned to cover fifty with him, but we ran out of time. If we had started sooner (or if he had flunked his junior year and given us twelve more months), then we would have covered the others. So, in some regards, I guess I am a nine-deposit failure for the rigid rule-keepers.

In any event, he told me he was fine with this book. So, I'm giving you a snapshot of what I did, how I did it, and why I did it, not because this is the perfect process, but because it might help you develop the best process for you and your son or sons.

I don't know any parent in the world who says it was a bad idea to spend intentional time with their children, and one of the best tools available to any parent is to spend alone time with a child discussing the things that matter to you and that you hope matter to them. So, if nothing else, maybe this book inspires you to do that more while giving you a framework for doing it.

As a general rule, frameworks really help us be more successful at whatever it is we're trying to do—dieting, planning a vacation, building a swing set, whatever. The framework for this book is really simple: Each chapter includes a story that drives home a succinct and specific point, followed by a few key insights to consider and questions to ask and answer. In some chapters, the insights are short (one sentence); in others, they are rather long and the opening illustration is short. That might seem like an inconsistency, but it reflects the way it happened in my meetings with Kile.

Kile and I also went through these deposits in a very random order, but I've arranged them into six categories—My Core, My Faith, My Heart, My Relationships, My Work, and My Future—for those who like that type of structure.

This is *a* framework, not *the* framework, for guiding some important conversations between fathers and their sons. Yes, it can work for fathers and daughters, mothers and sons, and mothers and daughters, but it's based on my conversations with my son, so it has the most direct application between fathers and sons. Regardless, you'll have to make it your own. That's why I call it more of a help-yourself book than a self-help book.

How you use this book is really up to you, but here's one suggestion. Read it with a pen, highlighter, or both. Take notes. Mark things of interest, things you agree with, things that apply to your family, things that don't. Then do one of two things based on your unique situation.

One, buy another copy for your son (if you feel strongly that he would read it in the right spirit). Re-read it along with your son and meet regularly to discuss the deposits. Personalize the examples, insights, and questions to fit the context of your son's life and your relationship with him. Skip deposits that don't have much application for your situation and add others that are better fits. Remember, some might be covered over one bagel; others might require a discussion that takes place over several visits.

Two, buy a journal for your son and use this book as a reference as you develop unique deposits that are more specific for your son and his life and more personal to you and the deposits you'd like to make. If you want, you can even buy a copy of the *41 Deposits Journal* made just for this purpose. My approach was usually to create an outline and spend an hour or two a week pondering and preparing, often within the context of my regular Bible study time. I like to put things into talking points, and I like to do a lot of theological checks. I enjoyed that process. As you prepare to share, of course, you will learn and grow yourself. Write your outlines and notes into his journal and give it to him later as a gift, or encourage him to bring the journal to your discussions and take notes as you chat.

Whatever you do, do it with love, and with the ultimate goal of strengthening the integrity of your heart-knot.

There are many ways to strengthen the integrity of the heart-knot with our children. This book provides one way. And there are many valuable wisdom lessons we can share with our children. This book provides forty-one of them.

Kile, to my great fortune, was a willing cohort in these meetings. He's an eager student of life. But he's not perfect. And neither am I. We had tough conversations where I shared transparently about my mistakes and the costs and consequences of making them. And he opened up about some of his struggles and challenges. It wasn't always easy, but working through the tension added integrity to our heart-knot.

He's a young adult now, and I often see evidence that he's drawing on the deposits from those breakfasts together. In many cases, I simply planted a seed that was watered and fed by other relationships and experiences. So, I can truthfully say the deposits are paying dividends in Kile's life. I can thankfully report that they have strengthened the integrity of our heart-knot. And I am a better and more joyful man because of our experience.

PART 1

My Faith

Faith is taking the first step even when you don't see the whole staircase.[1]

—Martin Luther King Jr. (paraphrased)

Fearing God

Fearing God is being certain that He is always present and His opinion matters most.

I once was a partner in a business that owned a small airplane. One of our partners had his pilot's license, so he did most of the flying. We saved money over commercial airfare, and, most importantly, we spent less time away from home and more time with our families.

In fact, it allowed us to institute an "eight-night quota"—an internal promise to one another that we would not spend more than eight nights a month away from home because of work. And, by the way, getting home at 1 a.m. didn't qualify as a night at home. We had to be home by dinner, or it didn't count.

Ron, the partner/pilot, had a saying he often quoted: "There are old pilots and there are bold pilots, but there are no old, bold pilots." And he lived by that statement. One day we were in Minneapolis when a snowstorm rolled in. My other partner and I wanted to leave, so we could get home for dinner. Ron voted to stay overnight in Minnesota. We pressed him—hard and repeatedly—but he wouldn't budge. Finally, he looked at us and said something like, "Here are the keys, guys.

You can go home. I'm not going until tomorrow. I'm not taking the chance."

We were outvoted 1-2 because neither of us knew how to fly an airplane and because Ron had a healthy fear of flying in bad weather.

Some of us have unhealthy, irrational fears. Taken to their extremes, these are known as phobias, and they prevent us from functioning normally—they can lead to dizziness, nausea, shortness of breath, or panic attacks.

In general, our healthy fears are of things that can bring us harm—flying in a snowstorm, a cougar that we come across during a hike, or a politician during an election cycle. (Just kidding on that last one . . . sort of.) But there is one thing we should fear even though it is the epitome of love: God.

It's a strange apparent contradiction, is it not?

We're told that fearing God is the beginning of all wisdom, but should we be afraid of an all-loving God?

When we really understand the nature of God, the answer is yes.

Think through the Scriptures. Any time a person has an encounter with God or an angel of God, the reaction is almost always fear. In fact, God or the angel of God almost always starts the conversation with, "Do not fear" or "Do not be afraid."

Why would anyone fear an all-loving God? At the heart of this type of fear is a true understanding that God is . . . well, God. The Author of the universe. The One who created the stars. The One who is all-powerful. The One who truly defines love and justice. The One whose presence we don't deserve to be in and whose standards we can never live up to on our own. The One who can do with us as He wishes—and we could never argue that His will is somehow wrong or unfair.

Remember when Jesus calmed the seas (Mark 4:35–41)? The reaction of the disciples was fear. They no longer feared the storm; instead, they trembled because they had a sober awareness that they were in the presence of God. Not just a higher version of themselves. Not just another religious guy. Jesus really was God in human form. Only God can manipulate the weather.

There should be a soberness in our hearts when we encounter God. Not a fear rooted in shame, guilt, and being scared, but a fear that ascribes the honor and majesty that are fully due Him.

If you ever played sports for a great coach, think of the tension in that relationship. You didn't fear the coach like you might fear an abusive parent or a cougar or a snowstorm. But you respected the coach for his knowledge and for his authority. When the coach gave an order, you knew to do it.

Fearing God is embracing the awe, respect, and submission that are due the Creator and Sustainer of life. We all wrestle daily with the question, "Who has the right to rule in our world?" Fearing God is fully surrendering that right to God. It's developing a clear understanding of the difference between God and you.

Pastor John MacArthur points out that "we ought to be shaken to our roots when we see ourselves against the backdrop of God's holiness. If we are not deeply pained about our sin, we do not understand God's holiness at all."[1]

Because the God we should fear is the God who actually loves us, our response should be obedience rooted in love and driven by stewardship. And, as Oswald Chambers noted, this same God calms all of our other fears like nothing else can.[2]

"The remarkable thing about God is that when you fear God, you fear nothing else," Chambers said, "whereas if you do not fear God, you fear everything else."[3]

Insights to Deposit

1. Fearing God is a natural and appropriate response to glimpsing His holiness and power.

2. Fearing God creates a posture of mind and heart that steers our conduct in the dark, secret moments of life.

3. Fearing God leads us to respect other people and treat them with dignity, without falling into the trap of seeing them as ultimate.

Questions

1. Why does the fear of God shape your integrity—not just what you do when others are around, but what you do in secret?

2. Where can you go to escape the presence of and certainty of God? (See Psalm 139:7–12.)

3. What's your understanding of God's holiness? And of your sinfulness?

4. Why would God want us to be constantly aware of His presence? What are the benefits of that?

Hearing God

God communicates; it's up to us to listen.

---

anley Beasley sat next to me on a flight from San Antonio to Denver and asked a typical Manley Beasley question. I was in my early twenties, and it was our first trip together during the year I spent working with the Hall of Fame evangelist. I was nervous and, at the same, excited about the yearlong learning journey in front of me.

"How much do you think our love offerings will be from the church we're going to this week?" he asked. "You write down a number, and I'll write down a number."

The look on my face told him I had no idea why he was doing this or how to answer his question.

"You believe God knows all, don't you?" he said.

I agreed.

"So, God knows the number. And do you think He knows it ahead of time?"

I agreed, again.

"Let's listen and see if God will tell us," he said.

I took a piece of paper, stared out the window, and began calculating the possibilities in my head. I thought about how many nights Manley was speaking, how many people would likely attend, and what the average gifts might be. Eventually, I came up with my best guess and wrote it down.

Manley, meanwhile, simply closed his eyes for a few seconds, then wrote his number down.

We put them in an envelope until the flight home, by which time I was burning with curiosity. When the time came to unveil the result, Manley showed me the check the church had written to his ministry. Then we opened the envelop. My guess was nowhere close—it was way high, as I recall. Manley's? It was exactly the same as the number on the check—down to the penny.

This wasn't about money or some name-it-and-claim-it approach to the gospel. This wasn't about someone being a super prophet with a more direct line to God walking among the rest of us mere humans. Manley was simply a man who had the gift of faith and who walked that out daily in his life and work.

Manley lived with seven terminal diseases, so imagine the faith it took to believe it when God was telling him that he would live to see his children's children. None of his children were even married at the time, but he believed and God delivered.

He had a strong muscle of faith, and it was harnessed to his ability to hear the voice of God. And while most of us don't have the extreme gifts that Manley was given, we all have a portion of faith and we all serve a God who communicates to us. It's up to us to listen.

The single most helpful instrument to aid our hearing God is to immerse ourselves in the Scripture. When we read the Bible, we hear God. But God is not limited to nor bound to only communicate with His children and the world through the canon of Scripture. Getting God's words into your heart will make hearing and interpreting His message so much easier.

We all have voices competing for our attention—voices of the enemy, voices of friends and family, voices of neighbors and coworkers, voices of the culture . . . Some speak discouragement, rationalization, condemnation, fear, and doubt. Others speak peace, love, and hope. The man who can sort out the voices around him (and the voices inside him) and detect the genuine voice of God is a man who is positioned to be strong until the last lap of life.

God communicates through the extraordinary on occasion, but also through the ordinary. He speaks in the thunder and the lightning, as well as in the still, small voice. He communicates through nature, people, actions, and, above all, Scripture.

Noted author Henry Blackaby was equally impacted by the life and work of Manley Beasley. He points out that God doesn't speak to give new revelations about Himself that contradict what's already been revealed in Scripture, but to apply His Word to your circumstances. "When God speaks to you," Blackaby says, "he is not writing a new book of Scripture; rather, he is applying to your life what he has already said in his Word."[1]

There's a security that comes with hearing God that supersedes everything else in life, because hearing God connects our faith to God and not the world around us or the emotions within us.

Insights to Deposit

1. Learn the language of God. Grab a Bible and fully engage in His communication with you. Jesus said, "My sheep hear my voice, I know them, and they follow me" (John 10:27).

2. When you can't or don't hear God, keep talking to Him. It's frustrating to feel like God is silent. It could be, as Rick Warren said, because we just aren't paying attention.[2] Or, as Dallas Willard said, it could be because "we do not in general want to hear it, that we want it only when we think we need it."[3] It could be that God is speaking and we don't like what He's saying, so we tune it out. Regardless, keep praying (talking with Him).

3. Listening to God doesn't mean we don't listen to people or common sense. There are countless examples throughout Scripture of God speaking to His people through His people. That's why we need godly friends. God also speaks to us through our own common sense at times. If you are thirsty and God isn't specifically telling you to avoid water, get something to drink.

Questions

1. Are you treating the Bible as God's timeless communication to you?

2. How hard is it to hear someone when you are nowhere near them?

3. What's the role of the Holy Spirit when it comes to hearing God?

4. How can you equip yourself to discern God's voice over other voices?

Resisting Temptation

*Temptation is the subtle yet attractive
bait Satan uses to lure us away from
God and His truth.*

T here are no guarantees in life that a father and son will share the same interests, much less that their greatest passions will align on the same hobby. So, I realize how blessed I am that Kile fell in love with fishing—my favorite hobby on the planet (nothing else is a close second).

We've been going to the White River since he was a little boy, and I suspected he was hooked, so to speak, when I got him a toy fishing pole one year as a Christmas gift. He clung to that thing like a security blanket, referring to it affectionately as "my blue pole." As he neared adulthood, Kile began to really get into fly fishing. Some of my favorite memories with him are of standing waist-deep together in the river below Beaver Dam, sun coming up over the tree line, fog slowly melting away on the water, and the flies we'd tied dancing in the current. We might have been fifty yards apart, but we were strengthening our heart-knot.

When it came time for us to talk about resisting temptation, the fishing metaphor was an obvious choice. And, naturally, we hung the discussion on James 1:13–15: "No one undergoing a trial should say, 'I am being tempted by God,' since God is not tempted by evil, and he himself doesn't tempt anyone. But each person is tempted when he is drawn away and enticed by his own evil desire. Then after desire has conceived, it gives birth to sin, and when sin is fully grown, it gives birth to death."

The Greek word used in that passage translated "enticed" is a fishing term. It's the same word used to describe a lure being thrown.

Fishermen ought to understand temptation better than anyone. You reach into your tackle box and try to find something that will entice the fish away from the deep water or the stump near the bank. There's an appetite within them that says, *I really want that fly.* And if they make their way to the top of the water and take the bait, they've been caught by their own desires.

Likewise, we're tempted, or lured, by our evil desires, not by God.

James identifies an important pattern. There's a temptation that awakens a desire, which leads us into sin, which leads to death. Only a relationship with Jesus offers forgiveness that overcomes death, and only a relationship with Jesus can create in us new desires less susceptible to temptation.

Temptations usually start in our hearts and minds when we see something that in and of itself is morally neutral or even good, but that we approach in an ungodly way because of our evil desires. That's why Proverbs 4:23 tells us, "Guard your heart above all else, for it is the source of life." Food is good for us. Gluttony is a sin. Sex is God-ordained. Sex outside of marriage is a sin. The bait looks good because something about it *is* good. That's what makes it bait. But it hides a deadly hook. It leads to sin when we give it over to the evil desires of our hearts.

Temptation itself is not sin. If you see a hundred-dollar bill in the chair after your friend has been over for a visit, you might become tempted. Or if you see a beautiful woman pass by your table at a restaurant, you might become tempted. Sin occurs when you take the bait and pocket the money or pursue the woman in an unbiblical manner. It also occurs when you coddle the sin—you may not have fully acted on it yet, but it's become a recurring visitor in your mind and heart—a visitor you refuse to kick out.

Thankfully, God equips us for our battles against temptations. We can, if we choose, put on the "full armor of God" (Eph. 6:10–18) and ground ourselves in our beliefs and convictions. Then when temptations come our way, we have something that protects and guides us. If we don't know what we believe and why, if we're not regularly in the Word, if we're not consistently seeking the guidance of the Holy Spirit through prayer, then we find ourselves with a heap of burning coals in our lap (Prov. 6:27) and wonder why we've been burned.

Because we are equipped by God, we can rest in the promise of 1 Corinthians 10:13: "No temptation has come upon you except what is common to humanity. But God is faithful; he will not allow you to be tempted beyond what you are able, but with the temptation he will also provide a way out so that you may be able to bear it."

In other words, just because we're tempted doesn't mean we have to end up like a plate of fish sticks.

Insights to Deposit

1. Temptation seeks to destroy you, not just inconvenience you. ("Be sober-minded, be alert. Your adversary the devil is prowling around like a roaring lion, looking for anyone he can devour." —1 Pet. 5:8)

2. Some temptations must be fought (pride, power, revenge, greed . . .); others you must run from (lust). ("She grabbed him by his garment and said, 'Sleep with me!' But leaving his garment in her hand, he escaped and ran outside." —Gen. 39:12)

3. Resisting and avoiding temptations strengthens you for future battles with temptations. ("We gain the strength of the temptation we resist."[1] —Ralph Waldo Emerson)

4. Temptations manipulate truth and hide a deadly hook within the attractive bait. ("The power of all temptation is the prospect that it will make us happier."[2] —John Piper)

5. The appropriate response to sin is repentance that leads to forgiveness. Don't stay hooked.

Questions

1. What's the difference between temptation and sin?

2. How has preparation helped you accomplish a challenging goal? How does that relate to preparing for temptations?

3. Why is it important that Christianity doesn't just reshape your actions, but reshapes your desires? How does that help you respond to temptation?

4. What roles do your friends play in leading you into or away from temptation?

5. What parts of your sinful nature are most enticed by temptations?

Worshiping God

If God is indeed the Creator and Sustainer of
life, then He is the one to worship.

One of the things all human beings have in common is that we all worship something. Martin Luther said, "Whatever your heart clings to and confides in, that is really your god."[1] It might be science, money, fame, the environment, a political or social cause, control, pleasure, approval, power, our physical bodies, or any number of other things in the world. Or it might be the one true God.

At its core, worship is giving the throne of our attention and energy to something. That focus becomes the most important thing in our lives, the thing that brings coherence, meaning, and fulfillment. That is the thing we crave and pursue.

Christian philosopher James K. A. Smith, author of such books as *You Are What You Love* and *Desiring the Kingdom*, points out that, "You can't *not* bet your life on something. You can't not be headed somewhere. We live leaning forward, bent on arriving at the place we long for."[2]

That "something" is defined by our fundamental view of God.

Theologian A. W. Tozer said, "What comes into our minds when we think about God is the most important thing about us."[3] We all have to decide if we believe that God exists. If so, can we know Him? Did God create us or did we create Him? Is He just a higher version of ourselves, or is He qualitatively different? Does He have the right to rule over our lives? Is He the center of this story we call life, or are we?

Worship involves the act of determining whether God is indeed real and worthy of our attention or if all the God talk is just another human crutch. If God is indeed the Creator and Sustainer of life, then He is the one to worship. In fact, He is the *only one* to worship.

Deuteronomy 6:4–5, known as the *Shema*, was a traditional morning prayer for the ancient Israelites. They would start their day by reciting it to affirm the object of their worship—"Listen, Israel: The LORD our God, the LORD is one. Love the LORD your God with all your heart, with all your soul, and with all your strength."

The most important decision we'll ever make in life is not *if* we will worship, but who and/or *what* we will worship.

Even if we acknowledge God as the only worthy object of our worship, however, we face the daily battle of actually worshiping God rather than the things of the world.

> A counterfeit God, according to Pastor Tim Keller, is "anything so central and essential to your life"[4] that losing it would make you feel like life is hardly worth living. Many of these things are good—our spouse, children, or career, for instance, aren't evil. But sometimes we can become so fixated on the people or things we love or that are worthy—even things

like morality, virtue, or ministry efforts—that we create a co-dependency. And, as Keller points out, co-dependency is really idolatry.

"An idol," Keller said, "is whatever you look at and say, in your heart of hearts, 'If I have that, then I will feel my life has meaning, then I will know I have value, then I'll feel significant and secure.'"[5]

On the other hand, everything about our lives can become worship. That includes our relationships with friends, children, and spouse, as well as our recreational hobbies and our careers.

Pastor Rick Warren points out, "Work becomes worship when you dedicate it to God and perform it with an awareness of His presence."[6] The same is true of other activities. Scripture says we can do everything to the glory of God. So, we can worship while eating, drinking, working, playing, learning, and more. Paul speaks to this in 1 Corinthians 10:31 when he says, "So, whether you eat or drink, or whatever you do, do everything for the glory of God."

Insights to Deposit

1. Worship is more than just singing a few songs in church. It is what we do with all of life. ("Present your bodies as a living sacrifice, holy and pleasing to God; this is your true worship." —Rom. 12:1)

2. Biblical worship is directing thought, love, and reverence toward God. ("Worship is giving God His true worth; it is

acknowledging Him to be the Lord of all things."[7] —Sinclair Ferguson)

3. We will forever fight the urge to worship things other than God.

4. You can only worship one master at a time. ("God is spirit, and those who worship him must worship in Spirit and in truth." —John 4:24)

Questions

1. What immediately comes to your mind when you think about God?

2. What things in your life, good or bad, compete for your worship?

3. What does worship look like in the daily activities of your life?

4. Describe what it means to worship God by directing each of these three things toward God: Your thoughts. Your love. Your reverence.

PART 2

My Core

The wise man does in the beginning
what the fool does in the end.

—Anonymous

Accepting Yourself

*Becoming settled and confident that you are
a one-of-kind creation from the genius of God
will anchor your life like few other things.*

A braham Lincoln and Stephen Douglas squared off seven
times in 1858 for formal debates when they were bat-
tling for a U.S. Senate seat in Illinois. During one of those
debates, Douglas accused Lincoln of being "two-faced" on the
issue of slavery. Without missing a beat, Lincoln famously
replied, "I leave it to my audience: If I had two faces, would I
be wearing this one?"

How many of us wouldn't change *something* about ourselves
if we could? We'd love to be taller, shorter, thinner, stronger,
smarter, more disciplined, better speakers, more talented sing-
ers, more athletic, or, well, whatever it is we aren't.

As an avid basketball player growing up, I dreamed of being
six feet, four inches tall. God had other plans. I never made
it beyond six feet; in fact, in recent years, I'm pretty sure I've
been shrinking. Research, unfortunately, confirms that men
can slowly lose an inch in height between the ages of thirty to
seventy (it's even worse for women, who can lose two inches).

There are certain things in life we can influence, and other things we can't. We have certain personality types, certain physical body types, and certain natural talents, skills, and aptitudes. We can maximize our potential with what we're given, but we can't create realities that aren't available or change who we fundamentally are.

Lincoln, who lost the senate seat to Douglas but was elected president two years later, had a sharp wit and a self-deprecating sense of humor that often revealed both his self-confidence and his self-awareness. He knew his strengths and weaknesses, and he was comfortable being himself. That's not always an easy balance to strike in our world, because our culture often promotes a false idea that accepting ourselves includes accepting and giving in to our sin nature or making excuses for our unhealthy or sinful choices.

Becoming settled and confident that you are a one-of-a-kind creation from the genius of God will anchor your life like few other things. It doesn't free you to change who you are or to justify living however you please; it frees you to discover God and all that He intends for you.

Joe White, the long-time president of Kanakuk Kamps, is known for telling parents the single most important thing they can teach their children is to be anchored in healthy self-awareness. Why? A healthy self-awareness frames all of life. It even frames how we relate to God.

People who have accepted themselves usually have a healthy self-awareness. They've come to understand what Paul meant in Romans 12:3 when he wrote, "For by the grace given to me, I tell everyone among you not to think of himself more highly than he should think. Instead, think sensibly, as God has distributed a measure of faith to each one." They've come to understand what he meant in 2 Corinthians 10:12 as well, when he said we "lack understanding" if we compare ourselves with others. And they've come to understand what the psalmist meant when he praised God because he was "remarkably and wondrously made" by God (Ps. 139:14).

Such Scriptures help us discover a healthy self-awareness where we don't think too highly or too lowly of ourselves. Thinking too highly places us above God. Thinking too lowly puts us below humanity. Thinking too highly makes us think we don't ever make mistakes, nothing is ever our fault, and we have no need for God. Thinking too lowly tells us everything is our fault, that we are a failure, unlovable, and beyond God's forgiveness.

People who have accepted themselves usually don't spend an inordinate amount of time and energy trying to be someone else or find their self-worth in pleasing someone else. They are comfortable in their own skin, self-aware enough to see their flaws, and eager to improve without a desire to become someone they're aren't. Then they are freed to become the best version of the person God created them to be.

Insights to Deposit

1. Eventually, you have to come to grips with who God made you to be and cultivate that. When you look in the mirror, see yourself as you really are and accept and even love yourself.

2. A lack of self-awareness is a blind spot that will affect everything in your life.

3. Accepting yourself doesn't mean becoming mediocre, accepting your sin, refusing to grow, or not trying to stretch yourself.

Questions

1. What is your biggest fear or insecurity about the way you look, your personality, or your giftedness?

2. Read Mark 12:30–31 and explain what you think it means about how you are to love yourself. "Love the Lord your God with all your heart, with all your soul, with all your mind, and with all your strength. The second is, Love your neighbor as yourself. There is no other command greater than these."

3. How does accepting yourself affect the way you see and relate to God? How does it affect the way you see and treat other people?

Loving Truth

*Love right, hate wrong, and be mature and
discerning on the gray matters of life.*

One of the teaching pastors at our church has an exceptional ability for driving home points with unique visual object lessons. One Sunday, for instance, he stood on the stage next to a table with a giant jar of Starburst candy on it.

"Lean to the person next to you and tell them how many pieces of candy you think are in the jar," he said. He gave everyone a few seconds to make a guess and then revealed the answer.

"There are 472 pieces of candy in the jar," he said. "Exactly 472. If you guessed 471, you were wrong. If you guessed 473, you were wrong. If you guessed *anything* other than 472, you were wrong."

His point: Some things in life are black and white issues. One thing is right and one thing is wrong. They are bound by truth.

Then he told everyone to tell the person next to them their favorite flavor of Starburst—red, yellow, orange, pink? After a few seconds, he laughingly declared the pink ones to be the tastiest.

His point this time: That is a different kind of question. It's a question of preference. And often we confuse truth with preferences.

Some things in life are black or white, right or wrong. All of life is not up to our preferences and opinions, which means our challenge often is to recognize right from wrong and act in obedience to do what is right. At the same time, much of life comes down to discernment in gray areas—the issues that are not outlined with 100-percent clarity in Scripture.

Truth is found in God's Word, and there's great value in that truth. The psalmist describes God's law as perfect, trustworthy, right, radiant, pure, enduring, reliable, altogether righteous, more desirable than gold, and sweeter than honey. And that's just in Psalm 19:7–10. No wonder he mediates on it "all day long" (Ps. 119:97).

Most of us look at truth through the lens of self-interest. The world tells us to follow our hearts, but Jeremiah 17:9 points out, "The heart is more deceitful than anything else, and incurable—who can understand it?" That's why we tend to look at what we want, then construct a "truth" that favors our feelings and desires. Instead, God calls us to look to Him for His absolute truths and for His help when discerning the gray areas.

First Corinthians 10:23–33 has been a guiding Scripture for me, especially when it comes to successfully navigating the gray areas in life.

"'Everything is permissible,' but not everything is beneficial," it says. "'Everything is permissible,' but not everything builds up. No one is to seek his own good, but the good of the other person" (1 Cor. 10:23–24).

Paul provided an example from his time regarding the food people could or couldn't eat. Then he says, "So, whether you eat or drink, or whatever you do, do everything for the glory of God. Give no offense to Jews or Greeks or the church of God, just as I also try to please everyone in everything, not seeking my own benefit, but the benefit of many, so that they may be saved" (1 Cor. 10:31–33).

Based on Paul's advice, when facing questionable matters of life, you can ask yourself the following:

1. Will it lead to peace and build up other people?
2. Is it beneficial and constructive?
3. Does it have the good of others at heart or is it self-centered?
4. Will it cause others to stumble?
5. Does it glorify God?

Separating truth from preference in today's world isn't always easy. In fact, it's often extremely hard. That's why it's so important to love the truth and pursue it. If we do, we're promised an answer (Matt. 7:7–8; Luke 11:9–10). Jesus said His disciples are the ones who "continue in my word" and told them, "You will know the truth, and the truth will set you free" (John 8:31–32). Ultimately, that's the guiding truth that matters most.

Insights to Deposit

1. Reading and digesting the Scriptures helps build a love for truth.

2. A heart for truth provides roots to ground you and wings to help you soar.

3. Pray for discernment to act wisely when things are not crystal clear.

Questions

1. Would you say truth is an endangered species in today's culture? Why or why not?

2. What is the role of the Holy Spirit as it relates to truth? (See John 16:13; Rom. 9:1; 1 John 4:1, 6.)

3. What's a decision you've made recently or are facing now that you believe is bound by truth over preference?

Taking Responsibility

We all own our responses to the
situations that come with life.

There was a sports production company that outgrew its headquarters in the late 1980s and moved its operations several miles away to a new facility. They used trucks to transport most of the furniture and equipment, but they decided to hire a helicopter to relocate their thirty-foot-wide satellite uplink dish. Shortly after the helicopter lifted off, however, something went wrong and the dish fell a few hundred feet, smashing to bits in a field.

The cause of the accident turned out to be a weak bolt, which the company's chief engineer—the man who had been in charge of the move—found in the wreckage. He did something odd with that bolt: He turned it into a keepsake. In fact, he kept it in his office for the rest of his thirty-year career. It was much more than a conversation piece—it was a visual reminder that he took personal responsibility for what had happened. The story became legendary among employees, and "Own the bolt" became a cultural mantra for showing courage and humility, and learning from mistakes.[1]

The story reminds me of a time when I was younger and I accidentally backed my car into another car in a parking lot. I jumped out to survey the damage. And even though it was minor, it was visible. As far as I knew, no one saw the accident, but I found a piece of paper, wrote down my name and phone number, and left the note on the other car.

No one ever called, but I was willing to own my mistake and accept the consequences. Why? Because taking responsibility was something my mother emphasized and modeled when I was growing up. And I suspect someone—or several someones—taught the same lesson to the engineer who owned the bolt.

Most people covet responsibility when it means they are getting more authority, more power, more control. What they really covet, however, isn't the responsibility; it's the authority, power, and control. But management guru Peter Drucker pointed out, "Rank does not confer privilege or give power. It imposes responsibility."[2] Or, as Ben Parker told his nephew Peter (a.k.a. Spider-man), "With great power comes great responsibility."[3] When it comes to mistakes, we often equate responsibility with blame, and we tend to hide from it, justify it, or shift it to others. Have you ever noticed how some people explain the accidents they caused by using the passive voice? "The paint spilled on the carpet" instead of "I spilled the paint on the carpet." But as the satirist P. J. O'Rourke pointed out, "One of the annoying things about believing in free will and individual responsibility is the difficulty of finding somebody to blame your problems on. And when you do find somebody, it's remarkable how often his picture turns up on your driver's license."[4] As the saying goes, when we point a finger at someone else, three fingers are pointing back at us.

Responsibility, however, is about more than owning our mistakes. It's about owning our response to everything in life—it's our "response ability" for owning our hard work, our education, the heavy loads we carry, the needs we see in front of us, the hard conversations, the authority we're given, *and* our mistakes.

Robertson McQuilkin understood the broader meaning of responsibility. When he was eight years shy of retirement, McQuilkin resigned the presidency of Columbia Bible College and Seminary (now Columbia International University) so that he could care full-time for his ailing wife. She had been stricken with Alzheimer's and was terrified to be without her husband. Some suggested that he put her in a nursing home, but he never gave that a thought.

"When the time came, the decision was firm," he wrote in an article for *Christianity Today*. "It took no great calculation. It was a matter of integrity. Had I not promised, 42 years before, 'in sickness and in health . . . till death do us part'?

"This was no grim duty to which I stoically resigned, however. It was only fair. She had, after all, cared for me for almost four decades with marvelous devotion; now it was my turn. And such a partner she was! If I took care of her for 40 years, I would never be out of her debt."[5]

Insights to Deposit

1. Don't make promises you don't fully intend to honor. ("When you make a vow to God, don't delay fulfilling it, because he does not delight in fools. Fulfill what you vow. Better that you do not vow than that you vow and not fulfill it." —Eccl. 5:4–5)

2. You will accept the consequences of your actions. The only question is when. Better to do it immediately. ("For each person will have to carry his own load. . . . Don't be deceived: God is not mocked. For whatever a person sows he will also reap." —Gal. 6:5, 7)

3. The things you've been given in life—talents, freedoms, relationships, authority, etc.—are gifts to be fully developed. ("From everyone who has been given much, much will be required; and from the one who has been entrusted with much, even more will be expected." —Luke 12:48b)

Questions

1. What are some things in your life for which you gladly and eagerly take responsibility?

2. What are some things or areas in life where you find it challenging to take responsibility?

3. Do you keep your promises? Why is that important?

4. Why is it sometimes hard to own your mistakes?

Asking Questions

Asking questions is an easy,
universal lever to learn and grow.

I magine you've twisted your knee while playing basketball and the pain is more than you can stand. You show up at the doctor's office, where you sit on the paper-covered exam table flipping through a three-year-old copy of *Field & Stream*. Thirty minutes later, the doctor and nurse enter the room.

"Okay," the doctor says to the nurse without so much as a *hello* to you. "This one's gonna need surgery to remove his gall bladder. Let's get that scheduled for next month."

The doctor then leaves, and the nurse tells you to pay your bill with the receptions. She'll call you later, she says, with the information you need for your surgery. Then she walks out the door.

As you hobble away to find another doctor, a million questions race through your mind, starting with this one: *Why didn't that quack ask me what was wrong?*

The progress of the world, not to mention an accurate diagnosis from a doctor, hinges on quality questions—questions for ourselves and questions for others.

Asking questions is how we learn and grow and how we learn to serve the world around us. As a consultant who helps CEOs, business owners, and entrepreneurs navigate high-level strategic issues, I can relate to the words of management guru Peter Drucker: "My greatest strength as a consultant is to be ignorant and ask a few questions."[1]

Consider Jesus. Jesus wasn't ignorant—in fact, He knew literally everything! But He still understood the value of questions. Early in my faith journey, one of my mentors challenged me to search through Scripture and capture every question asked by Jesus. I found more than a hundred, and I was amazed at how strategically and powerfully Jesus used questions. Some examples:

- "Do you believe that I can do this?" (Matt. 9:28)
- "Why are you afraid, you of little faith?" (Matt. 8:26)
- "What do you think about the Messiah?" (Matt. 22:42)
- "Do you love me?" (John 21:17)
- "Why do you call me 'Lord, Lord,' and don't do the things I say?" (Luke 6:46)
- "What do you want me to do for you?" (Luke 18:41)
- "Why do you look at the splinter in your brother's eye but don't notice the beam of wood in your own eye?" (Matt. 7:3)

Some of us are naturally curious and instinctively ask questions, but anyone can learn this powerful tool. It's not so much a character trait as a skill we can and must develop.

Start by remembering why it's important to ask questions. Here are just a few reasons:

- To learn something new
- To cause someone else to feel special or important
- To enable a person to discover answers for themselves
- To gain empathy through better understanding of another's view
- To influence or alter someone else's opinion or worldview
- To begin or strengthen a relationship
- To solve a problem.

Knowing why you're asking is important, but you also need to ask the right questions, in the right way, at the right time.

In Luke 11, Jesus tells a parable about a man who wakes up his neighbor in the middle of the night to ask for some bread to share with a traveler. The point of the story is that we often get what we want if we are persistent and bold, and that God will respond to our requests. But it's clear in the story that the guy asking for bread wasn't strengthening his friendship with his neighbor. His timing was horrible.

We also need to ask in the right way. That includes our tone of voice, our body language, and our level of sincerity. And it means that we don't start with the most personal questions, but neither do we spend all of our time asking about the news, weather, and sports.

Finally, we need to ask the right questions . . . questions with a purpose. Some experts will give you as many as twenty categories for questions, but I believe most fit into these three:

Conversational Questions—Asking people about themselves. These do not have to be profound, they just have to be sincere. Don't just ask for the facts; ask about the person's feelings or point of view on something.

Clarifying Questions—Looking for more meaning, answers, and insights. In general, the best questions are open-ended, and that's particularly true for clarifying questions. If the other person can easily answer with *yes* or *no*, then consider rephrasing what you're asking.

Rhetorical Questions—Asking a question so that others might answer it themselves. We all love self-discovery, and these types of questions help others find answers that they can own and use.

Insights to Deposit

1. Good leaders ask questions. ("The quality of a leader cannot be judged by the answer he gives but by the questions he asks."[2] —Simon Sinek)

2. Hungry learners ask questions. ("The important thing is not to stop questioning; curiosity has its own reason for existing. One cannot help but be in awe when contemplating the mysteries of eternity, of life, of the marvelous structure of reality. It is enough if one tries merely to comprehend a little of the mystery every day. The important thing is not to stop questioning; never lose a holy curiosity."[3] —Albert Einstein)

3. Great friends ask questions. ("He who asks a question is a fool for five minutes; he who does not ask a question remains a fool forever." —Chinese proverb)

Questions

1. Why do you think people often learn more by answering questions than by hearing a lecture?

2. Are you good at asking questions? How could you improve?

3. What are some examples of lessons you've learned by asking questions of someone else? Or by answering questions someone else has asked you?

Talking Straight

*Never underestimate the power of presenting the
right words, in the right tone, at the right time.*

———————————

The *Five Love Languages* became a best-selling book when it
came out in 1995, which was a long time ago, but still long
after my childhood. So, I'm confident my mother (GeGe)
didn't use that book as a resource to guide her parenting. And,
yet, she lived it.

My primary love language, per the book, is words of affir-
mation, and GeGe was fluent in that language. She constantly
injected the fuel of positive words into my tank. In fact, for as
far back as I can remember, my mother would sit next to me
when I was in bed and use words of encouragement to deposit
life, hope, optimism, and wisdom into my soul. She did this
well into my high school years, not just when I was a toddler.
And she had an uncanny ability to present the right words, in
the right tone, at the right time. By doing this, she created an
incredibly strong heart-knot between us, which is obviously
one reason I value relationships with my own children.

Words are powerful. God spoke the world into creation
(Gen. 1; Heb. 11:3), and Jesus is referred to as "the Word"

(John 1:1). But they also have a destructive power. Words can either be life-giving or life-draining. That's why the writer of Proverbs tells us, "The words of the wicked are a deadly ambush, but the speech of the upright rescues them" (Prov. 12:6).

Proverbs, indeed, has a great deal to say about the power of words. Take a spin through that book and here are some lessons you'll find:

Our words are a powerful force for good . . .

- When we speak truth. (Prov. 8:6–9)
- When we give good advice and wise counsel. (Prov. 10:20–21; 15:23; 25:11; 23:16)
- When we hold friends accountable and help them stay on the right path. (Prov. 17:10; 27:6; 25:11–12)
- When we bring encouragement and hope to someone who is discouraged. (Prov. 12:18, 25; 15:4; 16:24)

Our words are a powerful force for harm . . .

- When we are deceitful in flattery. (Prov. 28:23)
- When we slander and gossip. (Proverbs 10:18; 11:19, 13; 16:28; 17:9)
- When we brag and boast. (Prov. 16:18; 19; 27:2)
- When we are vulgar, profane, or dishonest. (Prov. 4:24; 15:4)

The most powerful words we can speak are about the love of God. When we share the story of Jesus, God works through us to change people. We can't change people. Our words can't change people. But God can use our words to bring people to transformative change. God brings about the change, but, as the apostle Peter tells us, our job is to share the reason for our hope, even at the risk of our own suffering.

> But even if you should suffer for righteousness, you are blessed," Peter writes. "Do not fear what they fear or be intimidated, but in your hearts regard Christ the Lord as holy, ready at any time to give a defense to anyone who asks you for a reason for the hope that is in you. Yet do this with gentleness and respect, keeping a clear conscience, so that when you are accused, those who disparage your good conduct in Christ will be put to shame. (1 Pet. 3:14–16)

Notice the words *gentleness* and *respect*. How we use our words matters. Being "right" about something isn't enough. If we say the right thing at the right time in the wrong way, we can't expect anyone to soak in the value. Part of speaking a language that others can comprehend is earning the respect to be heard and presenting the message with sincerity and love. Paul put it this way in Ephesians 4:29: "No foul language should come from your mouth, but only what is good for building up someone in need, so that it gives grace to those who hear." That's a universal love language.

Insights to Deposit

1. Our words tell others what is in our heart. ("Brood of vipers! How can you speak good things when you are evil? For the mouth speaks from the overflow of the heart." —Matt. 12:34)

2. Our words deliver life or death. ("Death and life are in the power of the tongue, and those who love it will eat its fruit." —Prov. 18:21)

3. Straight talk keeps us honest. ("If you tell the truth, you don't have to remember anything."[1] —Mark Twain)

Questions

1. What kind of speech is easiest for you and what kind is the most difficult?

2. Who in your world brings life and courage to you with their words?

3. What is the importance of Jesus being called the Word?

Being Authentic

Being authentic is discovering your creational
purpose and then daily closing the gap between
who you are and who you aspire to be.

It's hard to overstate the impact of the life of Howard Hendricks.

The man known as "Prof" authored or coauthored sixteen books, wrote countless articles, preached and taught in more than eighty countries, and spent sixty years on the staff at Dallas Theological Seminary. When he died in 2013 at the age of eighty-nine, the school estimated that Prof had personally taught more than ten thousand students.

I was one of them.

While he was widely considered the most effective Christian educator of his time, I remember him just as fondly for his impact outside of the classroom. In fact, one of the most enduring lessons he taught me came in a personal letter, not from a lecture. I don't recall the subject of the first handwritten note I received from Prof, but I'll never forget his signature. It was the same way he had signed all of his correspondence for decades:

"Without Wax, Prof."

That simple phrase in his signature line has served as an invaluable lesson and a guide in my life.

"Without wax" is derived from the Latin words *sin* (without) and *ceras* (wax). There's little proof that the phrase is the root of the English closing "sincerely" (*sin cersa*). But when Hendricks signed letters this way, he wasn't weighing in on an issue of etymology; he was subtly acknowledging the powerful imagery associated with the phrase.

Legend holds that unscrupulous ancient Greek and Roman sculptors would use colored wax to hide cracks and chips in their work. The wax hiding a crack in a vase or jar inevitably melted in the sun and wind. Whatever it stored then would seep out, wasted when the leak was exposed. So, those who refrained from the practice marked their pieces with the words "without wax" to signal the integrity of their work.

Prof adopted the phrase for his signature because it pointed to the importance of authenticity as a foundational principle for life and work in a culture consistently marked by shallowness or fakery.

God calls us to live without wax—to present ourselves to the world around us as we truly are, flaws and all. To be real. To be genuine. To be authentic. In 1 Timothy 1:5, Paul tells his protégé, "Now the goal of our instruction is love that comes from a pure heart, a good conscience, and a sincere faith." He was urging Timothy to build a faith that was without wax. Not perfect, but authentic.

We all have cracks. That's part of being human. Some cracks are moral weaknesses or failures. Others are insecurities, doubts, and fears. Am I smart enough? Talented enough? Experienced enough? We're not called to share every flaw with every person we encounter. But the circumstances of life cause all of us to regularly decide whether to practice a life of cover-ups and charades or a life of authenticity that closes the gaps, to the best of our ability, between what we say we are and what we really are.

It is certainly tempting to practice on-the-spot, surface patching of our chips and cracks. That shallow mending, however, just doesn't stand up to the pressures that life throws at us. Nor is it what God seeks from us.

The religious leaders during the time of Jesus weren't known for showing their flaws, but their flaws were no less real. Jesus, in fact, reserved his strongest criticism for these Scribes and Pharisees. They were pretenders. They were hypocrites. In Matthew 6 and 7, Jesus told his followers not to pray, fast, or give like those hypocrites, because they were seeking the praise of people, not God.

The word *hypocrite* just means a stage actor—someone who puts a mask over his face to pretend to be someone he's not. In the early days of theater, one actor would play several parts. He (or she) would just switch to a different mask when it was time to portray a different character.

The temptation today is to switch masks depending on our audience and always—*always*—use a mask that hides our flaws and highlights our best qualities. That's why so many photos on social media are of sunsets, beaches, puppies, and babies. There's nothing wrong with sharing the blessings of life, but there is a danger in taking it too far and creating a false narrative about who we really are.

The life of the hypocrite is not only deceptive; it's dangerous. The authentic life might not always look pretty, but it brings peace.

Insights to Deposit

1. Authenticity means being honest, vulnerable, and sincere.

2. Authenticity requires discretion; it resists the temptation to overshare or share inappropriately.

3. The easiest form of authenticity is to drop the mask and live as the same person with the same values regardless of the changing audiences or circumstances.

Questions

1. In what ways do you sometimes behave differently to impress a specific person or group of people?

2. Why are core values important to an authentic life?

3. Whom do you trust to call you out when you veer from the path of authenticity?

4. How has a display of hypocrisy caused pain for you or someone you know?

Understanding Valleys

*God leads us through the
unavoidable valleys of our lives.*

W alking through valleys is an inevitable part of the human experience. Think about it: Jesus told His followers that we "will have suffering in this world" (John 16:33). He didn't say we *could have* suffering or we *might have* suffering, but that we *will have* suffering. And the psalmist put it this way: "One who is righteous has many adversities" (Ps. 34:19).

The good news isn't that followers of Jesus go through life without troubles, but that we don't have to go through troubles alone. God will lead us through our troubles, and there's an eternal peace beyond this world.

It's worth noting the full versions of those two verses I just quoted, especially how they end. Psalm 34:19 says, "One who is righteous has many adversities, but the LORD rescues him from them all." And John 16:33 says, "I have told you these things so that in me you may have peace. You will have suffering in this world. Be courageous! I have conquered the world."

That's the *real* good news.

There is no such thing as a life with no valleys. None of us skip happily from one mountaintop experience to the next.

The Bible records the valley experiences of most of its major characters, and Hebrews 11 provides a tidy recap of many of them. You've no doubt been through your own low places. And I've certainly been through a few valleys during my life. I lost a business and had to walk through a long process of settling millions of debts in an honorable way. And one year my sister and my college roommate, who was one of my closest friends, both died unexpectedly.

Valleys come in many forms—a loss, a disappointment, a setback, an illness. They can result from something you did, something you didn't do, or something that happened to you that was outside of your control.

The question becomes, how do we walk through these valleys and learn from them?

I was in college in Mississippi when I heard a preacher named Ron Dunn teach on this topic, and he helped me set a framework for understanding and navigating the valleys of life. His talk on Deuteronomy 8:2, in fact, has become an anchor in my life.

Here's the verse: "Remember that the LORD your God led you on the entire journey these forty years in the wilderness, so that he might humble you and test you to know what was in your heart, whether or not you would keep his commands" (Deut. 8:2).

We often think the people of Israel just wandered aimlessly in the desert for forty years. Clearly, God led them. They didn't just stumble into a loop of clouds and confusion. They didn't lack direction. Their sinfulness played a role in putting them in the valley, but God led through the desert experience. He was engineering something divine.

The image of a desert is appropriate. It is dry. It all looks the same. It's tiring. It seems to last forever. It leaves you thirsting, not just for water but for hope. But in this verse, God seemed to be working in three specific ways in the people of

Israel. As He led them through the desert, God was trying to educate them, examine them, and empty them.

Educate them: by testing them, God taught His people lessons that would endure for generations. We all learn from times of testing, and the more we open ourselves to what we can learn, the better.

Examine them: God used this time to look into their hearts. Times of testing reveal our character. We all have sins of the heart. Fear, lust, pride, unhealthy independence, revenge, greed . . . God uses our valley or desert experiences to expose us to the sins we might be hiding from ourselves.

Empty them: forty years in a desert would be nothing if not humbling. God wanted His people to know they needed His help. We all have a desire for independence about us. The more successful we are, the more we can think we are the hero of our narrative, the reason for our success. God wants us to feel confident, but we always want an underpinning realization that we need to empty ourselves of our own self-sufficiency. Our confidence is in Him, not in ourselves.

Valleys feel bad. They hurt. Don't act like they aren't there. But regardless of how you got into the valley—by your sinfulness or through circumstances beyond your control—understand that there is some divine engineering at work as God leads you through it. You are not alone. God and other people are with you, and God has an agenda that ultimately yields your good and His glory.

Insights to Deposit

1. Valleys, for the follower of Christ, are always temporary, though they usually feel permanent. ("For I consider that the

sufferings of this present time are not worth comparing with the glory that is going to be revealed to us." —Rom. 8:18)

2. The greatest comfort in a valley is companionship with God and, very often, someone God is working through who is in your life. ("A person's steps are established by the LORD, and he takes pleasure in his way. Though he falls, he will not be overwhelmed, because the LORD supports him with his hand." —Ps. 37:23–24)

3. Valleys can be fruitful by Divine design. ("We know that all things work together for the good of those who love God, who are called according to his purpose." —Rom. 8:28)

Questions

1. Who have you seen go through a valley and handle it well?

2. Describe an experience you consider a valley in your journey through life. How were you educated, examined, and emptied by it?

3. How well are you equipped to remain grateful and hopeful during tough times?

Staying Pure

*Impure thoughts lead to impure
actions that lead to a dirty life.*

---

several years ago, an ice storm devastated our town and
the surrounding area. Oddly enough, I found myself more
concerned about the three mature maple trees in our front
yard than about the roof on our home.

Let me explain.

I'm a sucker for beautiful trees. One of the reasons I love
living in the Ozark Mountains is because the trees here are
so gorgeous in autumn. I also engineer trips to see clients out
West when the aspens are turning or to New England when
the maples are at their peak. I even have a photo of trees as my
screensaver.

I had planted these three trees as saplings and watched
them mature into full-grown adults. Each fall, I marveled as
their leaves burst into color—brilliant golds, fiery oranges, and
rich reds. These weren't just *any* trees. These were *my* trees.

Thankfully, the damage to my trees from that ice storm
was minimal.

One fall day as the trees across the Ozarks were bursting with color, I felt a wave of excitement as I drove toward a favorite corner of nearby Wilson Park. I was expecting to see the huge beautiful blazing orange maple that anchored a certain corner near Wilson Park, but, instead, I saw a tree that looked sick and barely had any color at all. I kept an eye on it through the winter and into the following spring. Then, over the summer, it just disappeared. One day it was there and the next . . . it was gone. It had died and the owner had decided to get rid of the eyesore.

I was so bummed.

Sometime later I was talking to a landscape architect who happened to know the story of that tree. It had caught a disease, he told me, become unhealthy, and died. They tried everything possible, but the impurities had rotted the tree from the inside out. A stump was all that remained of the beautiful tree that for decades had marked a corner of historic Fayetteville.

That tree is a great metaphor for moral purity. We must remain vigilant to keep impurities out of our hearts. Once a disease is planted in our hearts, it begins to grow. As it grows and takes root, we find ourselves acting in ways we regret. And those actions have consequences—some of them life-altering.

There's an old saying that's been attributed to everyone from English novelist Charles Reade to transcendentalist Ralph Waldo Emerson and from Chinese philosopher Lao Tzu to business author Steven Covey. It goes something like this: "Sow a thought, and reap an act; sow an act, and reap a habit; sow a habit, and reap a character; sow a character, and reap a destiny."

Conversely, there's a related quote from an unknown source that says, "If we reap what we sow, most of us should pray for crop failure."

The point is, our thoughts lead to actions that create habits, but bad habits result in negative consequences.

King David provides one of many biblical examples. Read 2 Samuel 11 and you'll find a story of a man who allowed his eyes to wander, which led to impure thoughts, which led to sinful behaviors, which caused him to abuse his power and commit multiple sins. Even though he was forgiven, he never escaped the consequences in this life of his actions.

Joseph, on the other hand, fled from temptation when Potiphar's wife attempted to seduce him (see Genesis 39). While he paid a heavy price because he was falsely accused and unjustly imprisoned, he maintained his integrity and protected his purity.

The world around us, of course, doesn't always see purity as a virtue. C. S. Lewis, in fact, pointed out in *Mere Christianity*, "Chastity is the most unpopular of the Christian virtues."[1] But once we allow impure thoughts to invade our hearts, we become like the diseased tree—it's harder and harder to recover as we rot from the inside out.

We all make mistakes. We will not be perfect. But when we mess up, we need to take drastic measures to rid ourselves of anything and everything that could keep a foothold in us. Too often, we wait until our behaviors are out of line with God's will before we recognize we've got a problem. What we need to do is recognize that impurity begins in our thoughts, so we can address it before it leads to sinful behaviors. We need the Doctor to show up when we have the impure thought, not just the impure action.

Insights to Deposit

1. Purity is an issue of the heart and mind first, then the body.

2. Purity is an ongoing internal civil war and is not easy at any age.

3. Purity is first tested in the little things: a look or double glance.

4. Purity can never be managed—"moderation" is not appropriate with impurity. Abstain, flee, or do both.

5. Purity acts as a good steroid for a clear conscience.

Questions

1. Why is purity—especially sexual purity—so hard for most guys?

2. What is your most challenging temptation with regards to purity?

3. Do Christians struggle less/more/the same as everyone else when it comes to staying pure?

4. What are the benefits of staying pure?

Living Daily

Learning to live one day at a time is about
embracing the joy of the ordinary.

A close friend of our family nearly died during the time period when Kile and I were meeting to discuss these deposits, and it led to some interesting conversations about the value of our ordinary moments in life.

Everyone familiar with our friend's situation, including all of the doctors, thought he would die very soon, but he didn't. After he recovered, well-meaning people would approach him and say something like, "God must have saved you for something extraordinary."

They meant to encourage him. But think about the pressure that statement puts on a man. It's as if they were saying, "I'm glad you lived. Now do something amazing. Otherwise, God might regret saving your life." Or, "Your life prior to your tragedy wasn't really that meaningful." Or, "Unless some electrifying output occurs connected to your life, it was a waste."

No one would ever say such things, but ironically, many of us put that type of pressure on ourselves and on others, even if we don't use those words. We don't mean to do it, but we slowly embrace the idea that nothing is really worthwhile if it's not amazing, wonderful, perfect, great, incredible, and otherwise worthy of going viral on the Internet. In doing so, we often strip from life the value, the worth, and the majesty of the ordinary.

Losing our appreciation for the ordinary leaves us in a state of perpetual dissatisfaction. If everything in life has to be super-sized, exaggerated, over-the-top, and the greatest of all time, then everything that falls short has little value. It drowns the sounds of simple joy. It blinds our eyes to pure good. It dulls our imagination to the true and the beautiful.

Some people who live in the moment, of course, are abdicating a responsibility to think around the corner. *I'm going to get my paycheck and spend it all today, they say, because I'm living for today!* That's just irresponsible. You still have to be a good steward. You need goals, and you should look to the future. But you have to balance that with the notion of living daily that Jesus described in Matthew 6:25–34. The net of these verses is that you shouldn't worry, but, instead, you should trust God one day at a time to care for you and provide for you. If He does it for His other creations (birds and flowers), He will certainly do it for His highest creation (man and woman).

Living daily isn't about accepting mediocrity in life, but about developing an everyday faith that keeps God front-and-center so we can embrace the joy of the ordinary.

Two books triggered my early thinking as a twenty-something about this type of everyday spirituality—*The Practice of the Presence of God* by Brother Lawrence and *True Spirituality* by Francis Schaeffer.

"Think often on God, by day, by night, in your business and even in your diversions," Brother Lawrence wrote. "He is always near you and with you; leave him not alone."[1]

Francis Schaeffer, meanwhile, said, "A quiet disposition and a heart giving thanks at any given moment is the real test of the extent to which we love God at that moment."[2]

God is present and engaged in your life all day every day. He is not sitting around waiting for Sunday, so He can meet you at church. He doesn't show up during an early morning Bible study and then disappear when you leave for school or work. There is no sacred/secular split. The greatest assignment and challenge in life is not to do some mission out of the ordinary, but to invite God into every moment of your life and work.

I think the power and dignity of the ordinary life are what Martin Luther King, Jr. had in mind when he said, "If it falls your lot to be a street sweeper, go on out and sweep streets like Michelangelo painted pictures; sweep streets like Handel and Beethoven composed music; sweep streets like Shakespeare wrote poetry; sweep streets so well that all the host of heaven and earth will have to pause and say, 'Here lived a great street sweeper who swept his job well.'"[3]

Wake up and announce to yourself and the world—"This is the day the LORD has made; let us rejoice and be glad in it" (Ps. 118:24).

Insights to Deposits

1. Slow down and value the ordinary.

2. Trust God one day at a time, but dream of (and act on) what could be.

3. Welcome each day as a fresh new start with Jesus, knowing that it is a not a license to ever knowingly do wrong.

4. Remember, God desires to commune with you every day of your existence, regardless of what is happening. ("Because of the LORD's faithful love we do not perish, for his mercies never end. They are new every morning; great is your faithfulness!" —Lam. 3:22–23)

Questions

1. How have you seen the presence of God in the ordinary?

2. What are two or three daily habits you can instill that will remind you of God's presence throughout the day?

3. How would you describe the balance you need between a healthy ambition to succeed in life and doing ordinary tasks to the glory of God?

Embracing Manhood

Every young boy must navigate
his journey to manhood.

A number of men shaped my life as father-figures when I was growing up. Nine, actually. And the first one I can remember was Mr. Cherry.

I'm not sure I ever knew Mr. Cherry's first name. He was an adult, and I was a skinny grade school kid who was looking for ways to earn some cash to pay for things like a bike, a basketball, and a week of summer camp. When I went looking for lawns to mow, I ended up at Mr. Cherry's door and he put me to work for the better part of two consecutive summers.

Mr. Cherry never sat me down for a one-on-one talk about manhood, but he taught me as much about it as almost anyone. He modeled what it looked like, and he made it clear that he expected to see it in me. He taught me lesson after lesson about responsibility, quality, working quickly, excellence, fairness, integrity, and the concept of mentoring—all without ever mentioning any of those words. He shaped my view of work, but, more than that, he helped develop my earliest thinking about what it means to be a real man.

It took me years to realize Mr. Cherry wasn't hiring me to mow his lawn because I was the best option, but because he had empathy for me and my mom and he wanted to make a tangible contribution to my life.

Every young boy must learn what it means to be a man and navigate his journey to manhood. That is not always easy or simple; it wasn't for me, even with great mentors like Mr. Cherry showing me the way. And it certainly isn't easy or simple for guys today.

Some things haven't changed and never will. The transition from boyhood to manhood involves setting aside our childish narcissism and immature ways as we accept the responsibilities of adulthood, do the hard things that come with life, overcome challenges and adversity, and invest in important relationships.

The concept of manhood, however, is more confusing and unstable than ever. We have men who have abused the role of being a man and spoiled the image. And we have a culture that has unraveled the core concepts of sexuality and gender, to add confusion. Our world seems to be fine with strong femininity, but not strong masculinity.

The truth is, all men are different. We don't all know how to hunt and fish. We aren't born with an extensive knowledge of cars and sports. We don't all have deep voices and thick beards. But none of that means we should reject a stripped-down version of manhood, even if authentic manhood might seem countercultural or old fashioned.

Ultimately, every man needs a battle to fight, an adventure to live, and a beauty to rescue. That age-old triad, popularized most recently in books by John Eldredge, is part of the manhood wiring, not just something we pick up if we grow up in a certain home with certain surroundings. These three needs are written in the hearts of all men, says Eldredge: "That is what little boys play at. That is what men's movies are about. You just see it. It is undeniable."[1]

How we live out that wiring can and should look different for different men, but we are missing out on all that it means to be an authentic man if we run from life's battles, shy away from risks that take us on new adventures, and fail to care for the women in our lives (especially, for married men, our wives).

Robert Lewis, the founder of Men's Fraternity, says pursuing this type of healthy, biblical manhood involves four things, which he outlines in *Raising a Modern-Day Knight*:

1. Rejecting passivity,
2. Expecting God's greater reward,
3. Accepting responsibility, and
4. Leading courageously.

Again, these aren't easy. Adam embraced passivity (and failed to rescue his beauty) when he stood silently beside Eve as she ate the forbidden fruit. Satan skillfully tells us to embrace our selfish reward, to shift blame when things go wrong, and to redefine courage as bluster and entitlement rather than a heart-based character trait. But when we actively pursue and invest in those traits, we are able to discover the true essence of manhood, and to reap the rewards that come from living as real men.

Insights to Deposit

1. Biblical manhood calls us to lead and to follow.

2. The company we keep either reinforces or bankrupts our investments in manhood.

3. Manhood isn't about being in control but about living as a servant leader.

Questions

1. How do you see manhood portrayed in characters in modern movies or television shows, and how is that similar or different from biblical manhood?

2. Who are the Mr. Cherrys of your life who are investing in or have invested in how you understand authentic manhood?

3. What do each of these qualities look like in your life:

    1. Rejecting passivity,
    2. Expecting God's greater reward,
    3. Accepting responsibility, and
    4. Leading courageously?

Fighting Perfectionism

Perfectionism is nothing less than idolatry.
Only God is perfect.

---

om Peters and Bob Waterman believe the most effective leaders have a bias for action. In their dated, yet best-selling book, *In Search of Excellence*, they pointed out the value of what they called a "ready, fire, aim" approach. It doesn't work in every situation a leader will face, and sometimes you end up shooting yourself in the foot, but more often than not it leads to action, which leads to progress.

For leaders who are perfectionists, however, "ready, fire, aim" is a challenging concept to adopt. They tend to prefer "ready, aim, aim, aim, aim, aim, aim . . ."

The fight against perfectionism isn't something everyone faces. It's more of a personality thing. Some people live on the other side of the spectrum. They lack the ambition or motivation to work toward their best, so they yawn and settle for mediocrity. So, this deposit might not seem that applicable to some people.

We live in a highly competitive world, however, and many kids feel intense pressure to live up to some unachievable standards—to make "perfect" grades, wear the "perfect" clothes, have the "perfect" bodies, hang out with the "perfect" group of friends, get accepted into the "perfect" college, or be whatever else "perfect" looks like in their particular world.

I remember reading Kile a long quote from *Be a Perfect Person in Just Three Days!*, a children's book by Stephen Manes that makes the point that it's okay to be less than perfect.

"Congratulations!" Manes wrote. "You're not perfect! It's ridiculous to want to be perfect anyway. But then, everybody's ridiculous some-times, except perfect people. You know what perfect is? Perfect is not eating or drinking or talking or moving a muscle or making even the teeniest mistake. Perfect is never doing anything wrong—which means never doing anything at all. Perfect is boring! So, you're not perfect! Wonderful! Have fun! Eat things that give you bad breath! Trip over your own shoe-laces! Laugh! Let somebody else laugh at you! Perfect people never do any of those things. All they do is sit around and sip weak tea and think about how perfect they are. But they're really not one-hundred-percent perfect anyway. You should see them when they get the hiccups! Phooey! Who needs 'em? You can drink pickle juice and imitate gorillas and do silly dances and sing stupid songs and wear funny hats and be as imperfect as you please and still be a good person. Good people are hard to find nowa-days. And they're a lot more fun than perfect people any day of the week."[1]

The world gives us mixed messages about perfection. This quote, which has been attributed to everyone from basketball players Wilt Chamberlain and Charles Barkley to statesman Winston Churchill, sums up what many of us feel when pushed toward perfection: "They say that nobody is perfect. Then they tell you practice makes perfect. I wish they would make up their mind."

In Matthew 5:48, Jesus calls us to, "Be perfect, therefore, as your heavenly Father is perfect." But He is talking about an effort to be holy, to have integrity, and to live fully in the sight of God, not about judging yourself too harshly and failing to realize that God gives you grace to keep going when you mess up.

Scripture, in fact, makes it clear that we're not perfect, which is exactly why we need grace from a perfect God. First John 1:9 says that "if we confess our sins to him, he is faithful and just to forgive us our sins and to cleanse us from all wickedness" (NLT). Later in that same epistle, John says, "My dear children, I am writing this to you so that you will not sin. But if anyone does sin, we have an advocate who pleads our case before the Father. He is Jesus Christ, the one who is truly righteous" (1 John 2:1–2 NLT).

Rather than obsessing over perfection, Scripture calls us to pursue biblical excellence.

Consider the difference:

> A perfectionist compares himself to others, which leads to pride or discouragement. A pursuer of biblical excellence embraces the unique design, standard, and calling God has on his life.

A perfectionist can't handle failure and over personalizes criticism. A pursuer of biblical excellence sees beyond his failures and still has authentic hope in Jesus' work for and in him.

A perfectionist is motived to do well out of fear, guilt, or insecurity. A pursuer of biblical excellence is motivated out of gratitude and service to God.

A perfectionist sets unreal goals and expectations for himself. A pursuer of biblical excellence sets goals for excellence and leaves the results to God.

A perfectionist usually sees the glass as half empty and lives in a world of caution and can't. A pursuer of biblical excellence usually lives in a world of "maybe it will work out and the sun is shining somewhere today, so I might as well act like it is shining on me!"

A perfectionist doesn't understand or practice biblical grace. A pursuer of biblical excellence is defined by the God of radical grace, the God who did something for him that he could never do for himself, and that he doesn't deserve.

Insights to Deposit

1. God calls us to glorify Him by pushing ourselves to maturity and excellence, not the futile pursuit of physical or spiritual perfectionism.

2. Perfectionism starts in the head and heart. It is a subtle step of believing and then digesting the lie that we could ever completely separate ourselves from sin in this life.

3. Our significance and satisfaction in life come from accepting God's claim on our lives, then following that with passion, not by chasing perfectionism.

Questions

1. How would you define perfectionism?

2. Why do some people seem to struggle more with perfectionism than others?

3. How can you spot someone struggling with perfectionism? How do you spot it in yourself?

4. What are the feelings and thoughts that usually ride along with perfectionism?

Developing Perseverance

*Staying power sustains us along
the faith-journey of life.*

The United States celebrated its bicentennial birthday in 1976, and people around the country marked the occasion in all sorts of creative ways—picnics, parades, speeches, plays, fireworks, air shows, fun runs—you name it, and people were likely doing it.

I signed up, albeit reluctantly, to participate in one such event, and it pushed me to my limits. Some friends had agreed to make a cross-country run from the Alamo in San Antonio, Texas, to the capital in Washington, D.C. The idea was to find sponsors whose contributions would raise money for charity and then to make public appearances along the way. For some reason I no longer remember, one of the three had to bow out of this monthlong marathon. So, the other two called and asked me to take his place.

"I'm out," I said.

"Pray about it," they said.

"No thanks," I said.

"What else do you have to do this summer?" they said, knowing I was a high school coach and teacher with the summer open, so to speak.

"Well," I said. "Nothing. But no thanks. I'm out."

They were persistent, however, and I didn't have a good enough alternative to back them down. So eventually I committed to join their team, and three days later I was on a Friday afternoon flight from Memphis to San Antonio.

On the ensuing Monday, we laced up our running shoes and took off, tag-teaming our way up and down America's roads for more than 1,600 miles. We stopped to speak to church groups, meet with governors, sleep, and eat. But we had distance goals for each day, so mostly we ran . . . in the sun . . . in the rain . . . during the day . . . and sometimes at night. It took thirty-two days, but on July 4, 1976, we arrived in Washington, D.C., right on schedule.

I was in good shape at the time and ran regularly, but I hadn't trained for this type of endurance test. It wore me out physically, pushed me emotionally, tested me mentally, and stretched me spiritually. And while there were times when I wanted to quit, stopping never was an option. I took pride in doing my part and finishing strong, and my friends and I pushed and encouraged one another throughout the journey.

I've leaned into that experience often in the face of life's challenges because it taught me all sorts of lessons about perseverance. Some social scientists claim that perseverance (or grit, to use the more current term) is the single most common trait among consistently successful people. I don't know how true that is, but I do know that staying power is important in life. And like most things of value, it doesn't come easy.

Why do we want to quit when the going gets tough? All kinds of reasons: Maybe we lack a deep commitment on the front end. Maybe we are dogged by a voice in our head from the past. Maybe we don't have a compelling "why." Maybe our core is gripped by fear. Maybe our goals are too tied to other people's expectations.

Regardless, we need a solid understanding of perseverance if we're going to develop it for our good and God's glory. We are assured that we will face troubles in our lives (John 16:33). We typically don't know when they will come or what form they will take, but we can expect the unexpected. So, we're wise to plan for life's challenges. That means we save money for the proverbial rainy day. That means that we invest in our faith to keep it strong. That means we put on the armor of God to withstand temptations (Eph. 6:10–18). And that means we develop perseverance.

I've often heard it said that ideas depend on enthusiasm, but bringing those ideas to life in the real world depends on perseverance. Williams Shakespeare put it this way in *Henry VI*: "Many strokes, though with a little axe, Hew down and fell the hardest-timber'd oak."[1]

In other words, *perseverance is a difference-maker.*

The apostle James said, "Consider it a great joy, my brothers and sisters, whenever you experience various trials, because you know that the testing of your faith produces endurance. And let endurance have its full effect, so that you may be mature and complete, lacking nothing" (James 1:2–4). In other words, *perseverance is a character-builder.*

The author of Hebrews said, "Therefore, since we also have such a large cloud of witnesses surrounding us, let us lay aside every hindrance and the sin that so easily ensnares us. Let us run with endurance the race that lies before us, keeping our eyes on Jesus, the source and perfecter of our faith. For the joy that lay before him, he endured the cross, despising the shame, and sat down at the right hand of the throne of God" (Heb. 12:1–2). In other words, *perseverance is an appropriate response to God's love for us.*

Author Mary Anne Radmacher said, "Sometimes courage is the quiet voice at the end of the day saying, 'I will try again tomorrow.'"[2] And the apostle Paul told the Galatians, "Let us not get tired of doing good, for we will reap at the proper time if we don't give up" (Gal. 6:9). In other words, *perseverance finds hope and hangs on to it.*

And C. S. Lewis said, "If you're on the wrong road, progress means doing an about-turn and walking back to the right road; in that case, the man who turns back soonest is the most progressive."[3] This reveals the danger of wrongheaded perseverance. In other words, *perseverance can be twisted into self-centered stubbornness.* It can be a chain that holds us too long and drives us into fantasy thinking. It can make us try to solve the unsolvable, lead us for miles down the wrong road, or keep us treading water when we should ask for help.

But God-centered perseverance—grit motived by the right reasons and lived out in faith—transcends the types of battles we face. It serves us in times of failure, boredom, and mediocrity. It lifts us from stress, depression, and anxiety. When the odds against us make the task seem impossible, it inches us closer and closer until we arrive at our destination. As Charles Spurgeon said, it got the snail to the ark.

The world doesn't object to our being a Christian for a short season. It just doesn't want us to stay with it to the end. The Christian journey has a start, middle, and end. Perseverance is the thing that sustains us along the journey.

Insights to Deposit

1. When you fail and disappoint yourself, seek forgiveness then get back in the game. ("Perseverance is not a long race; it is many short races one after the other."[4] —Walter Elliott)

2. Staying power is rooted in faith, not just self-determination. ("We are able to persevere only because God works within us, within our free wills. And because God is at work in us, we are certain to persevere."[5] —R. C. Sproul)

3. Perseverance is an individual trait but it can be fueled by community and team. ("A true Friend unbosoms freely, advises justly, assists readily, adventures boldly, takes all patiently, defends courageously, and continues a Friend unchangeably."[6] —William Penn)

Questions

1. Who are the friends who challenge you to do more than you think you can do, but who also encourage you to reach those goals?

2. Why is faith relevant to perseverance?

3. What role does passion for a cause or goal play in perseverance?

4. What roadblocks typically tempt you to give up on a worthy goal?

PART 3

My Heart

Whatever your heart clings to and confides in, that is really your god.[1]

—Martin Luther

Learning Contentment

Contentment is learning to say enough is
enough and really believe it and practice it.

A friend and his wife were in Tegucigalpa, the largest city in Honduras, when they were asked to help paint a local family's home.

While most of the people on the trip were working in an inner-city church that was hosting a medical clinic, my friends and a few others grabbed some buckets of white paint and a few rollers. They climbed into the back of a box truck for a bumpy ride that took them about a mile away before stopping in the middle of a dirt street. From there, they walked about fifty yards down a beaten path to a house built out of unpainted scrap wood that stood perilously on the side of the steep mountain.

They spent the morning painting and enjoying a conversation with the husband and wife who lived there. They laughed, told stories about their families, ate the food the wife cooked, watched her wash the dishes in a basin outside the house, and wrote the husband's favorite verse (Jer. 33:3) on the side of the home in English.

The family owned almost nothing more than the clothes they were wearing, yet they were a beautiful picture of contentment. They had a quiet joy that wasn't defined by their circumstances, but that was evident in their voices and mannerisms.

I know another couple who are both successful doctors. Years ago, I went to their home with a friend who was asking them for a donation to a worthy cause. They didn't know him but agreed to the meeting because they knew me (although back then they didn't know me all that well).

When the presentation ended, I was shocked that they not only wrote a check, but a check for a substantial amount. I found myself mentally going through all the other things they could have done with their money and realizing they must have come to a place where they were content with a certain lifestyle. They had drawn a line.

I've spent my entire life around people who have more "stuff" than I. And for a good bit of my life, I've had more "stuff" than most other people in the world. Here's what I've noticed: wealth and the accumulation of stuff have nothing to do with contentment. I know people who have multiple homes, fancy cars, and private jets, but who lack contentment. And I know people who can't afford bus fare to get to work, but who are content.

Contentment is learning to say enough is enough and learning to really believe and practice it. It is an elusive quality, because we often want the things we don't have and ignore or minimize the things we do have.

Of all the qualities you can learn in life, finding contentment regardless of your circumstances is one of the most stabilizing foundations you will ever construct. This is actually what Paul meant when he wrote, "I am able to do all things through him who strengthens me" (Phil. 4:13). Paul wasn't talking about winning football games or getting a dream job—he was talking about how he had "learned the secret of being content—whether well fed or hungry, whether in abundance or in need" (Phil. 4:12).

I don't know of another virtue that grounds us better in today's unsatisfied society. Without it, your heart swirls between voices in your head, marketing messages by the millions, the never-ending appeal to "treat yourself," and the self-driven desire to live for only today, not for eternity. With it, you can experience peace and joy regardless of your circumstances and you can freely make choices that benefit others; without it, you will never be satisfied.

The places where I have found the most meaningful instruction about contentment are in a short portion of a letter Paul wrote to his understudy, Timothy, and then another phrase from a letter to a start-up church at Philippi.

To Timothy, Paul wrote, "But godliness with contentment is great gain. For we brought nothing into the world, and we can take nothing out. If we have food and clothing, we will be content with these" (1 Tim. 6:6–8).

Remember, Paul had *learned* the secret. He wasn't born with it. Contentment is a virtue that we learn. That means it is available to all of us, not just to a special subset of people. And it also means we have a responsibility to learn it.

So, how do you learn it?

Here are a few guidelines I've found helpful.

- You will never learn contentment unless you know the difference between essentials and nonessentials. In an age of consumption, it's often difficult to draw a line between what you need—for yourself, your

family, and your businesses—and what you
simply want.

- You will never learn contentment if you
can't appreciate what you have been given
and stop comparing yourself and your possessions to others.

- You will never learn contentment if you
can never say *no* and *enough is enough.* You
have to learn to draw a line and say, "I don't
need another pair of shoes or fishing rod or
car or house or boat."

Contentment, of course, is not just about money and possessions. It also can be about status—am I content with my job
title or with the number of "likes" my posts get on social media
or the role I play on a sports team or the attention I receive
when hanging out with friends? Ultimately, contentment is
about embracing your dependence on God and realizing that
He gives you all that you truly need.

C. S. Lewis wrote about contentment in the context of
money, but his statement applies to anything that puts our
desires above God's discretion. "One of the dangers of having a
lot of money," Lewis wrote, "is that you may be quite satisfied
with the kinds of happiness money can give and so fail to realize your need for God."[1] True contentment comes only when
we realize and rest in our need for God.

Insights to Deposit

1. Contentment is a learned character trait that runs against our personal and cultural wiring.

2. Contentment can only come when we learn to separate the bare necessities of life from the never-ending desire for more.

3. Contentment expands your scope to others and learns to trust that what God has given you is enough.

Questions

1. What makes contentment elusive and hard to learn?

2. How is your contentment influenced by society, marketing, and other people?

3. What are your most prized possessions?

4. Name something you have learned to do that could be an example of learning something like contentment?

Practicing Rest

*Humans were designed to balance work,
play, and rest; when we ignore rest,
we end up in dangerous territory.*

———————————————

iwa Sado was a thirty-one-year-old political reporter for a public broadcasting company in Japan when she died from a cause that's become all-too-common in her culture: *karoshi*.

Sado was the picture of an ambitious, talented, young journalist. But her work consumed her, defined her, and, eventually, killed her. Her work schedule, according to investigators, included one month with 159 hours of overtime and just two days off.

She died of heart failure, but the official cause of death—what the Japanese call *karoshi*—literally means, "overworked death." In 2015 alone, Japanese officials attributed 189 deaths to overwork. Ninety-three were suicides and the other ninety-six were from heart attacks, strokes, and other illnesses related to overwork.[1]

Japan, of course, isn't the only place where people overdo work. A *Harvard Business Review* study released in 2018, for instance, found that CEOs work, on average, 9.7 hours per weekday, and another 3.9 hours on the weekends. They also average 2.5 hours of work per day when they are on vacation.[2]

In our hyper-connected, highly competitive world, it's easy for anyone, not just CEOs and ambitious journalists, to fall into the habit of nonstop work. In fact, our society even glamorizes it. But while a strong work ethic is essential in life, an inability to turn off our work is, at best, unhealthy and unsustainable, and, at worst, life threatening.

Biblical rest, however, is about more than not working so we can take a nap. There's a spiritual concept to true rest. God created the Sabbath, blessed the Sabbath, and commanded us to remember the Sabbath and keep it holy (Gen. 2:2; Exod. 20:8). And Jesus described the spiritual element of rest in Matthew 11:29–30 when He said, "Take up my yoke and learn from me, because I am lowly and humble in heart, and you will find rest for your souls. For my yoke is easy and my burden is light."

True rest is a salve for our souls found only in Jesus. The true Sabbath, then, comes only when we're surrendered to God, trusting not in our own (un)finished work, but in the finished work of Jesus on the cross. Then we can rest in our souls, knowing that there is nothing we can add that will increase or decrease our favor with God.

At the same time, biblical rest absolutely involves a pattern that takes us away from work.

Think about this: God created the heavens and the earth in six days, but there's no indication that it was a six-day, nonstop type of job—not for God. He spoke everything into existence, something He could have chosen to do in one moment rather than over six days. We aren't sure how much of each day He spent on the speaking part and how much He spent looking over that day's work. But we do know that He did no work whatsoever on the seventh day, establishing a pattern of balance for us to follow. We work (and rest) for six days, then take a tangible break in the weekly work routine for a Sabbath.

One Old Testament scholar pointed out that the Sabbath is first and foremost about work stoppage, not worship. "It is about withdrawal from the anxiety system of Pharaoh," he said, "the refusal to let one's life be defined by production and consumption and the endless pursuit of private well-being."[3]

The Sabbath is a breaking of the routine of work. You cannot get away from that. It's a shutdown. It means to turn it off, to lay it down, to walk away—to stop, cease, and desist from work for a spot of time. It's not complicated to understand, but it is a bear to apply.

It takes faith to walk away from work knowing there are things to be done—not faith in our ability to catch up the next week, but faith that God *really is* the God of everything in our lives. Real rest—Sabbath rest—is literally activating our faith and trusting that God will take care of us when we stop whatever we're doing and fully connect with Him.

Insights to Deposit

1. Work and rest must be woven together. They are interdependent concepts. God commands us to do both, so they are a partnership of divine making that are intended to go together.

2. There are seasons when we have to be out of a healthy work-rest rhythm—tax season for the CPA, finals season for the college student, the new business launch for the entrepreneur, the first few weeks or months after a baby is born, the harvest

time for a farmer, etc. But no one can live a long, fulfilled life if they are constantly out of a healthy rhythm.

3. Not keeping a Sabbath, as Andy Crouch puts it, is idolatry. "Instead of remembering, enjoying and celebrating the goodness of the true God," he writes in *Playing God*, "we make ourselves gods, pressing ourselves to ever greater feats of self-sufficiency, and doubtless lapsing, exhausted, into slothfulness when our busyness overwhelms us. All idolatries, left unchecked, end up consuming us. A sabbathless life ends up with neither true work nor true rest, but with frantic and ineffective activity punctuated by couch-potato lethargy."[4]

Questions

1. Where do you find the greatest rest? Do you have a particular routine, setting, or habit that brings rest?

2. Why is rest so crucial?

3. What seasons in your life challenge you the most when it comes to practicing biblical rest?

4. Why is resting a confession that God is God and you are not?

Chasing Balance

We can't know it all, be it all, or do
it all. But we can experience balance
within our personal limits.

———————————

friend of mine began working from home a few years ago,
so he set up an office in one of his spare bedrooms. To save
on expenses as he started this new phase of life, he turned
an old computer desk into the centerpiece of his work world.
It was just the right size for a laptop and a photo of his wife,
but not much else.

Within a few months, files, papers, books, and other
assorted work resources covered the desk. Stacks began to
grow like flowers in the spring. After about two years, my
friend went out and bought a regular-sized desk. He added an
external monitor, spread out some of his stacks of stuff, and
even had room for the bobblehead collection that previously
had been banished to a closet.

It sure would be nice if adding capacity to our cluttered
lives was as easy as buying a bigger desk. But the reality is that
we're all limited by the size of the desktop we're given. We
might have more capacity than some, but we all have limits.

And if we don't manage our capacity well, things stack up, eventually get out of balance, and inevitably topple over.

We all have twenty-four hours in a day. Even Jesus, while on Earth, lived within the confines of time. So, we have to make choices and trade-offs, and it's an ever-evolving daily battle. The idea that we can chase it all and have it all in life is, simply put, bunk. We can't know it all, be it all, or do it all. But we can experience balance within our personal limitations.

Balance, however, isn't about evening up some mythical scales. Rather, it's about recognizing the responsibilities of our daily calling and managing them in healthy, productive ways that align with our capacity. That means we have to learn to juggle the demands of life. As author Simon Sinek put it, "There is no decision we can make that does not come without some sort of balance or sacrifice."[1]

My personal approach to this includes a habit I developed decades ago. Every Sunday night, I make a list before I go to sleep of things that can be done and the things that must be done during the coming week. I write it on paper and always restrict myself to one page. It covers both my personal and my work lives. I force myself to sort and prioritize the demands and opportunities that are coming my way. And often I have to make tough decisions about what and who will *not* get my time and attention.

Dave Ramsey, whose finance management program has helped thousands get out of debt, tells the story of being hounded by debt collectors early in life when he and his wife faced bankruptcy. One thing they did was prioritize who they would pay each week with the income they had. Food and shelter were their top priorities, then their list continued to other things. When they ran out of money, they drew a line. One day he was on the phone with a particularly aggressive collector.

"Dude, I would really like to pay you," Ramsey said, "but I can't."

"Why?" asked the collector.

"You're below the line," Ramsey said.[2]

Sorting through the demands on our lives helps us decide what we will put above the line and what will have to wait for another day—or be dismissed forever.

For some personality types and for some people in certain stages of their faith journey, a strictly hierarchical approach is most comfortable. God first, family second, friends third, work fourth, and so on. A holistic approach, however, puts God in the center with self, others, work, hobbies, community, service, and other demands orbiting and getting different degrees of attention in different seasons of life.

To juggle those things well, we have to learn how to sort through our opportunities and filter our priorities so that we're focused on the right things at the right time. Life is dynamic. Our top priority today might fall below the line two years from now. But we often get locked into doing something even when life and circumstances change. Peter Drucker once said, "There is nothing so useless as doing efficiently that which should not be done at all."[3]

When we understand our capacity, we can push the limits occasionally, but we're also more likely to discover our natural rhythms for work, rest, and play. And when we keep God at the center regardless of competing priorities, we're quicker to recognize when our desktop is overloaded, and we can make corrections before everything topples over.

Insights to Deposit

1. No matter how high your ceiling, there is still a ceiling. Everyone has a capacity limit.

2. Everyone's capacity is different, so don't fall into a comparison trap with the people around you.

3. Seeking first the kingdom of God is the top priority when chasing balance (Matt. 6:33).

Questions

1. What does it mean to your view of balance to know that God spent six days creating and one day resting?

2. What three or four things compete the most for your time right now?

3. What word best describes the pace of your life right now, and why: Balance? Harmony? Chaos? Dysfunction? Other?

4. Describe your desktop of life. What are the limits of your personal capacity and how close to capacity are you right now? Keep in mind that you could be beyond capacity, or you could have too much empty space.

Reflecting Joy

Joy is both an emotional and spiritual state.

---

incoln Markham went beyond Google for his elementary school science project, and it changed his family's future. His project would explain what's inside five sports balls, and he and his dad, Dan Markham, decided it would be fun to actually cut the balls in half. When they did, they recorded it on video. Then Dan put the videos on YouTube so Lincoln's classmates could see them.

You probably know, or at least can predict, what happened next. Turns out, there was a huge market for videos showing a cute kid and his dad having fun cutting stuff open to see what was inside. The five videos posted in January 2014 turned into a "what's (in)side?" YouTube channel with more than 4.5 million subscribers and partnership agreements with multiple well-known brands.[1]

The videos reveal what we instinctively know: what's inside matters. And it's not just true of products; it's also true of people, especially when it relates to joy.

Joy is both an emotional and spiritual state, and it reflects what's going on with our inner self. As human beings, we're made of more than flesh and bones, so you can't examine the soul with an autopsy. But you do have some control over what happens at your core, and that will determine if you are truly joyful.

Joy is listed among the fruit of the Spirit (Gal. 5:22), which means it's a Christian virtue, and something that is developed and grown, like an apple or a pear. But fruit grows on a tree or vine, and the fruit of the Spirit doesn't grow without a connection to the vine of Christ.

The formula most people use for finding joy is really a formula for experiencing happiness. And the formula for finding happiness is really a formula for experiencing favorable circumstances. But joy is grounded on spiritual realities, not just circumstances. C. S. Lewis said joy is the "serious business of heaven."[2] And John Piper said, "Christian joy is a good feeling in the soul, produced by the Holy Spirit, as He causes us to see the beauty of Christ in the word and in the world."[3]

When we think of the ancient Israelites, we might think about how often they grumbled and lost their way. They lost their joy or lacked joy because of their circumstances. But there are plenty of examples where they reflected joy, and one of my favorites is the dedication of the rebuilt wall around Jerusalem.

Nehemiah 12:27–43 describes the scene. Here's the short version: "At the dedication of the wall of Jerusalem, they sent for the Levites wherever they lived and brought them to Jerusalem to celebrate the joyous dedication with thanksgiving and singing accompanied by cymbals, harps, and lyres. . . . Then I brought the leaders of Judah up on top of the wall, and I appointed two large processions that gave thanks. . . . On that day they offered great sacrifices and rejoiced because God had given them great joy. The women and children also celebrated, and Jerusalem's rejoicing was heard far away."

First, we learn that joy is God-centered. The joy in this scene came to the people as a result of being in the very presence of God, gathered as His people, giving thanks to Him.

Second, we learn that joy comes in remembering God's faithfulness. Not so long before this scene, the wall was a heap of rubble, the city empty, and the Word of God neither heard nor understood. Now they gathered to celebrate God's protection and provision in finishing what most thought to be an impossible task. Remembering His faithfulness fosters joy.

Because joy is God-centered and spiritual, it's not about us or the circumstances around us. So, it comes from serving others and having gratitude regardless of the circumstances. As Leo Tolstoy said, "Joy can only be real if people look upon their life as a service and have a definite object in life outside themselves and their personal happiness."[4]

But what about those times when life stinks? When the friend betrays you or your sports team loses on a last-second buzzer-beater or the dog literally eats your homework? What about all of those times when you mess up or when life just isn't fair?

That's when we *really* get a chance to reflect joy. Unfavorable circumstances are merely teaching tools that prepare us for something better. As James 1:2–3 tells us, "Consider it a great joy, my brothers and sisters, whenever you experience various trials, because you know that the testing of your faith produces endurance."

Paul tells the Philippians to "rejoice in the Lord always. I will say it again: Rejoice!" (Phil. 4:4). He doesn't say, "sometimes" or "when life is good." *Always*. That's because we should see the bigger picture. Every day is a day the Lord has made, so we should rejoice and be glad in it (Ps. 118:24). Followers of Christ are the only people who can have joy not *because* of our circumstances, but *regardless* of our circumstances. Why?

Because of what we know to be ultimately and eternally true of us in Christ.

Insights to Deposit

1. Joy is deeper than happiness. ("Weeping may stay overnight, but there is joy in the morning." —Ps. 30:5b)

2. Joy (and a lack of joy) is contagious. ("A joyful heart is good medicine, but a broken spirit dries up the bones." —Prov. 17:22)

3. Joy is a reflection of our obedience. ("Rejoice in the Lord always. I will say it again: Rejoice!" —Phil. 4:4)

Questions

1. Why is joy different than happiness?

2. What are your greatest sources of joy and contentment?

3. When do you feel like your joy is being stolen—by your own actions or attitudes, by circumstances, or by other people?

4. How can you reestablish joy in your heart in times when you are tempted to despair?

Finding Peace

*Peace is the ability to be calm, steady, and joyful
during hard, confusing, and troublesome times.*

O ne day I went out for what I now call my "Forrest Gump"
run. I was in graduate school in Texas—young, single, and
in the best physical shape of my life. I ran regularly, but
not just to stay in shape. It was my time alone to clear my head,
pray, and wrestle with some of life's biggest questions.

On this particular run, I spent a good bit of time talking
to God about the fact that I had grown up without a father at
home. I wouldn't say I had a deep "father wound," but I had
some pain and confusion in my heart. And for whatever reason,
that pain and confusion dominated my thinking as I made my
way down a random road leading southwest out of Fort Worth.

After a few miles, I paused for a moment next to a fence,
stared at the giant herd of cattle feeding in the pasture, and
literally asked God to settle my heart and give me peace about
my future. Then I returned to the road and began to run.

I ran. And ran. And ran. And ran.

The next thing I knew, I had traveled twenty-one miles
away from my apartment. There were no cell phones back

then, so I had to find a phone and call a friend to come pick me up, because there was no way I could run back. I was exhausted—physically, mentally, and emotionally. But I also was at peace. God had settled my heart.

It's easy to smile and be happy when everything's going well. But when life turns upside down—when you are wrestling with the baggage of your childhood, when your best friends disappoint you, when you are in an airplane that's bouncing through a thunderstorm, when you get laid off from work, when you learn a family member has a terminal disease, when the circumstances around you seem hopeless or confusing—well, it can be really hard to find peace.

My good friend Tommy Van Zandt was forty-nine years old and the picture of good health when his life was flipped by a tragic accident. He was happily married with two great kids. He was a partner in a successful commercial real estate company. And he was a high-energy guy who always was on the go. Then he fell from a ladder, suffered a broken neck, and became a quadriplegic.

Tommy says that before the accident, the idea of being paralyzed and unable to take care of himself and his family would have made him depressed, anxious, and scared. And, yet, he and his wife and their family live today with an incredible peace.

"God's grace was with me and still is," Tommy wrote in *Flipped*, a book by his brother-in-law about their family's ordeal. "I just have a sense of peace about me that I'm going to be okay and my fate is in God's hands. God doesn't cause bad things to happen; but God's there to pick you up when bad things do happen. So, I had this peace about me, and I still do."[1]

People who have peace in the middle of life's troubles are unmistakable. A deep, internal, abiding personal peace is really undeniable. We've all been around people who have a calmness and settledness, and it's not because they don't have tough things going on. They stick out and are a magnet to others because they have peace *despite* the tough times they are experiencing.

Our culture promotes peace, but its version of personal peace is typically deceptive and dangerous. It overpromises and underdelivers. It tries to convince you that . . .

- Peace is about having stuff you don't have. *"If only I had this friend or that job or that stuff, I could have peace."*
- Peace is about experiencing something you have yet to experience. *"If I could go here or there, I could have peace."*
- Peace is about not having any troubles. *"If only I didn't have these hassles and headaches, I could have peace."*

Real peace is the ability to be calm, steady, and joyful during hard, confusing, and troublesome times.

That's the type of peace Paul references in his letter to the Philippians, because it allows you to actually rejoice when the world around you says you should be bitter, depressed, or despondent.

> Rejoice in the Lord always. I will say it again: Rejoice! Let your graciousness be known to everyone. The Lord is near. Don't worry about anything, but in everything, through prayer and petition with thanksgiving, present your requests to God. And the peace of God, which surpasses all understanding, will guard your hearts and minds in Christ Jesus. (Phil. 4:4–7)

This is exactly the type of peace Jesus offered His disciples after spending three years with them, and it's exactly the type of peace He offers us. While we might not have to run twenty-one miles to find it, we do have to ask. And when we seek it and truly listen, He will provide it.

Insights to Deposit

1. Peace is more about receiving a gift than achieving a state. ("Peace I leave with you. My peace I give to you. I do not give to you as the world gives. Don't let your heart be troubled or fearful." —John 14:27)

2. Peace is possible in times of chaos, trouble, and disaster. ("I have told you these things so that in me you may have peace. You will have suffering in this world. Be courageous! I have conquered the world." —John 16:33)

3. Peace is daily leaning on the sustaining promises of God. ("You will keep the mind that is dependent on you in perfect peace, for it is trusting in you. Trust in the LORD forever, because in the LORD, the LORD himself, is an everlasting rock!" —Isa. 26:3–4)

Questions

1. Who is the most at-peace person you know?

2. What does someone with a lot of peace look like?

3. Why is personal peace such a bedrock?

4. What makes experiencing peace a hard thing?

PART 4

My Relationships

*We think like the people we most
admire and need. Everyone belongs
to a community that reinforces
the plausibility of some belief and
discourages others.*[1]

—Timothy Keller

Picking Friends

Shared experiences allow iron to sharpen iron.

---

ile was in the second grade when a few friends and I began what became one of our favorite heart-knot traditions—an annual father-son canoe trip on the Buffalo River. As soon as school was out, usually in early June when the spring rains had the river at just the right level, we'd take off for a long weekend of camping, grilling, fishing, canoeing, storytelling, and manly grunting.

The first year, if my memory is correct, there were five dads and five sons, with each father-son tandem in their own canoe. As the years went on, it looked like a rag-tag armada had taken over the river. The group kept growing and growing, and we had great fun paddling, bonding with other dads and boys, sharing meaningful conversations around a campfire, cooking and eating great food, getting swamped, jumping off cliffs, chasing snakes, catching fish, navigating rapids—you get the picture.

As you might expect, when the boys got older they began to pair up in the canoes, often leaving us dads behind until they took a break on a gravel bar and skipped rocks until we caught up. The same thing happened with the campsites. The boys ended up going to one end and the dads to the other. Independence was needed and granted.

These trips were fun, but also deeply meaningful. As dads, we wanted our boys to spend time with men who were committed to following Christ so they could see us (hopefully) model biblical manhood. We wanted them to hear how we talked about things like our wives, our friends, our work, and our God. We wanted them to learn how to get along with other guys, to support one another even when it wasn't easy, and to develop empathy and respect for one another. And we wanted them to forge friendships with other boys of character—young men they could lean into, lean on, and lend a hand to during the journey of life. We believed, as Proverbs 27:17 tells us, that "iron sharpens iron" and, as Proverbs 13:20 advises us, that the "one who walks with the wise will become wise, but a companion of fools will suffer harm."

These bonding events created and deepened friendships, resulting not only in great memories but lifelong relationships built on a shared history and deep, mutual trust. They helped them learn four powerful lessons about relationships that Solomon shares in Ecclesiastes 4:9–12.

One, great friends turn work into a rewarding experience. ("Two are better than one because they have a good reward for their efforts." —Eccl. 4:9)

Whether it's building a campfire, navigating rapids, or competing together as a team in a late-night trivia contest, working with someone helps strengthen a relationship and the results almost always are better than one can achieve alone. Friendships forged on our river trips often spilled over into partnerships on things like school projects or on sports teams.

Two, great friends support each other when they stumble. ("For if either falls, his companion can lift him up; but pity the one who falls without another to lift him up." —Eccl. 4:10)

We aren't designed to do life alone, and life can feel particularly lonely when we experience failure. Having someone there to pick us up when our canoe gets swamped or when we trip up on a hiking trail provides the encouragement and motivation we need to keep going. We also need friends we can trust to tell us the hard truth and hold us accountable when we cause our own fall. "Better an open reprimand than concealed love," says Proverbs 27:5–6. "The wounds of a friend are trustworthy, but the kisses of an enemy are excessive."

Three, great friends offer comfort during lonely and desperate times. ("Also, if two lie down together, they can keep warm; but how can one person alone keep warm?" —Eccl. 4:11)

Practically speaking, the more guys in the tent during a cold night on the river, the warmer the temperature in the tent. It might not smell so nice, especially when the guys are teenagers, but it will be warmer than sleeping alone. The bigger principle from this verse is that we often find ourselves in desperate situations, and we need a close friend—not just an acquaintance—to stick close to us and see us through. We need different levels of friendships. Everyone can't be our best friend, but we need a few deep friendships for the toughest of times. Proverbs 18:24 puts it this way: "One with many friends may be harmed, but there is a friend who stays closer than a brother."

And, four, great friends provide practical protections when you are attacked or overwhelmed. ("And if someone overpowers one person, two can resist him. A cord of three strands is not easily broken." —Eccl. 4:12)

Proverbs 17:17 tells us, "A friend loves at all times, and a brother is born for a difficult time." We know that we will face troubles in life (John 16:33), including some unfair and unwarranted attacks. Our friends stand with us.

Those guys went different directions as college and adulthood beckoned, but several of them remain connected, and all of them understand the value of authentic friendships and how to build them.

Insights to Deposit

1. Investing in friendships will cost you time and energy. Invest in them anyway.

2. Building empathy requires trust and that trust sometimes is betrayed. Build it anyway.

3. Pouring love, respect, and grace into someone won't always produce a close friendship. Pour them in anyway.

Questions

1. What qualities do you look for in a friend whom you would trust with your most difficult challenge in life?

2. Why is it important to have a friend who holds you accountable to high standards and who isn't afraid to tell you when you're acting like a jerk? How do you respond to such a friend?

And, if you have to hold another friend accountable, how do you deliver your message?

3. What are some ways you can take a casual friendship built largely on a fun activity and help make it more meaningful?

4. What's the role of transparency in developing a deep friendship?

Loving People

Loving people is a soul-satisfying,
divine endeavor.

My friend Louie Giglio understands what it means to love people. All people.

You, me, that guy at the intersection with the sign asking for money, that girl who is pregnant and doesn't know who the father is, that CEO who was convicted of laundering company money, that mother who can't keep her three kids under control at Walmart, that obnoxious guy on social media . . . You know . . . all of us.

I was spending time not long ago with my friend Louie Giglio when he said something I've heard him say many times before: "If you are not comfortable on a subway, you are not going to be comfortable in heaven."[1] He wasn't referring to the temperature on the train or how overcrowded the cars might be. He was talking about the vast diversity of people you find on a typical subway ride.

As humans, we often become too narrow in our affections for others. We love only people who are like us or who feed our egos. Followers of Christ are no exception. But Jesus loves all people, and He calls us to love others just as He loves us.

That sounds nice, and it's easy to nod our heads in agreement with the sentiment. But, man-oh-man is it hard to put into practice, especially when we really consider what it means.

As a young man living in Memphis, I had a life-altering experience about what it *really* means to be loved by God and to love other people. It happened one morning during my daily run. Maybe I was thinking about some big screw-up in my personal life. Maybe I was reflecting on the messages I'd been hearing Chuck Swindoll teach on the radio about David and his sins. Maybe it was a combination of the two. I don't really know. But as I jogged through the streets of the Bluff City early that morning, I became overwhelmed by the notion of just how much God *really* loves me.

When I say overwhelmed, I mean literally overwhelmed. I'm not immune to tears, but I'm not one of those human faucets either. I probably wouldn't cry at your wedding, and I seldom shed tears during movies. It's just not the way I'm wired. On this morning, however, my legs got weak, I dropped my body onto a park bench, and I balled like a hungry baby. I sat there for more than an hour, and I cried—not out of pain or fear or frustration, but out of awe. I intensely felt the magnitude of God's love—the depth of it laid against my own depravity and failure—like never before.

There were a million reasons in my mind as to why God shouldn't love me, a million reasons why He should say, "Enough. You've had plenty of chances. You blew it. I'm moving on without you." Yet, Romans 8:38–39 makes it clear that God doesn't dump us because of our mistakes (or because of anything, for that matter).

Sitting and sobbing on that bench, it hit me that God loves everyone that deeply. They don't deserve such love. I don't deserve such love. But God loves everyone in this incredibly powerful way. All people.

My experience that day altered the way I think about other people. They aren't projects to fix. They aren't failures for me to judge. They are people to love. It was convicting and challenging. It still is.

Loving others isn't all smiles and acceptance. It has edges like truth, discipline, knowledge, and accountability.

Some people really struggle with the idea that God loves them. That's why I have been such a fan of *The Furious Longing of God* by Brennan Manning. It hammers home the notion that God's extravagant love is a life-altering epiphany.

Some people have a hard time accepting love from others. They bristle and think it is weakness. And some people (most of us?) have a hard time loving the people we don't really like. It is easy to love people who are friendly, who serve our needs, or who feed our ego. It's harder to love the jerks, the malcontents, the socially awkward, or anyone else who takes us out of our comfort zones. And, by the way, that can include the people closest to us. Often it is easier to demonstrate random acts of kindness (paying for the guy in the tollbooth behind us) than to love those who are right in the thick of life with us.

Yet, God says we all are "remarkably and wondrously made" (Ps. 139:14). Remembering this helps lay the foundation for loving others in light of who they are rather than how they behave.

The trump card of the gospel is love. Love for God. Love for the people God puts in our world. This is such a deep, powerful, and challenging idea that—fair warning—discussing this deposit with your son might take several weeks. But I can't think of any deposit more worth spending so much time on.

God is love. That, quite simply, means everything.

> And we have come to know and to believe the love that God has for us. God is love, and the one who remains in love remains in God, and God remains in him. (1 John 4:16)

Insights to Deposit

1. Loving people is rooted in embracing the love God has for us. First John 4:19 tells us "We love because he first loved us."

2. We all need to be loved, and we all need to give love. Mark Twain hit on this when he said, "Kindness is a language that the deaf can hear and the blind can see."[2]

3. Loving people is always measured in actions, not merely words or heartfelt emotions.

4. Embracing love isn't always easy.

5. Loving people is life-giving.

Questions

1. How does it change your understanding of life to know that you are loved by God?

2. Describe someone you love. What is that love anchored to?

3. What is the hardest thing about loving someone very close to you?

4. What are a few things that make it hard for others to love you?

Receiving Help

Be hungry for advice from wise friends.

Charles Cornwallis and George Washington typically took very different approaches when it came to running their war councils during the American Revolution. And never was that more apparent than on a cold January evening in the early stages of the war when the two generals plotted their next moves during a winter campaign in New Jersey.

It was several weeks after Washington's forces had famously crossed the icy Delaware River for an epic battle in Trenton, New Jersey. Now he was back, and his army had taken a defensive position along the southern side of Assunpink Creek. Cornwallis, meanwhile, led his much larger army on a long march through the muddy snow of New Jersey with the purpose of recapturing Trenton. They arrived late in the day, briefly and unsuccessfully engaged Washington's army, then pulled back to rest and regroup.

Some advisors to Cornwallis recommended an immediate nighttime attack, but the general decided to wait until the next day. His troops were worn out, and he had his prey trapped—the icy river on one side and the massive British army on the other. They would make quick work of their rag-tag enemies in the morning, he reasoned.

Retaking Trenton was even easier than Cornwallis expected. When his army charged in the next morning, they discovered the Continental army was gone. Washington had ordered a stealth and strategic retreat down a path given to him by the locals who had been called in to share their insights during the war council the night before. By the time the British realized what had happened, the Americans were well on their way to victories in and around Princeton.

Rather than dictating a solution and holding stubbornly to his plan, Washington had framed the problem, sought advice from people he respected, and made a decision on the best course of action.

The moral: Be hungry for advice from wise friends.

Let's break that down.

Be Hungry . . .

When we are hungry, of course, we look for something to eat. And when we develop a reputation for looking for advice—eagerly, as if it's critical to our survival—it's amazing how many people willingly agree to share what they know.

Proverbs 15:31 says, "One who listens to life-giving rebukes will be at home among the wise."

When we are hungry for advice, we pursue it. We don't passively wait for someone to push their wisdom on us; we ask for it with humility and honesty. And we don't toss it aside when we get it. We listen intently. We don't respond defensively. We don't argue. We ask questions and try to understand.

It's arrogant to think we see everything clearly and correctly as we skate through life all by ourselves. We all have blind spots. So, we need to be strong enough, mature enough, and confident enough to ask for help when we need it. And, for that matter, we need to be open to others speaking into our lives even when we think we don't need it.

For Advice . . .

Advice is nothing more than guidance that's recommended. It isn't a dictate from on high. It's a suggestion that we can take or leave.

When a police officer turns on the lights and siren behind you, he's not advising you to pull over. He's demanding it. When he says you might want to replace that burned out brake light, he's giving you some advice. You can ignore it or take it. And if you ignore it, you take the risk and reap the consequences. But what if he pulled you over and wrote you a ticket without telling you what you'd done or how to avoid another ticket in the future? Or what if the ticket had that information, but you tossed it in the trash?

Without input and advice, we are doomed to a life of self-deception, pride, and a lack of self-awareness. And that is a lethal concoction.

From Wise Friends . . .

Advice from a fool is not only worthless; it's dangerous. It doesn't lead us out of trouble, but into more. That's why it's so important to surround ourselves with wise, trustworthy counselors. And when our normal circle of friends lacks the experience or knowledge to see us through some new and challenging situation, we have to be wise enough to look elsewhere.

Washington didn't just ask his generals for advice; he asked farmers, too.

Proverbs 24:5–6 tells us that it's more important to be wise and knowledgeable than strong, "for you should wage war with sound guidance—victory comes with many counselors."

Gathering valuable insight and wisdom from a collection of trusted advisors provides us with collective wisdom that can reshape how we think and behave—if we're willing to ask for it and receive it.

Insights to Deposit

1. Guard your heart and mind against unhealthy independence—thinking you can do life alone with no outside help.

2. Learn to ask for and receive guidance from others. Don't just tolerate outside help; be hungry and enthusiastic for it.

3. Seek advice from people you trust, who share your values, and who bring wisdom and knowledge to their insights. Filter their advice through your own understanding of biblical truth.

Questions

1. Who are three to five people you immediately turn to for advice?

2. Who should be on that list but isn't, and why? Whom should you think about removing from the list?

3. How willing are you to ask someone who knows you well to tell you about your personal faults and blind spots?

Standing Alone

There are occasions in life when you must stand alone against the current of the crowd.

Movies are filled with story lines where someone—usually the hero or someone in need of a hero—steps forward against overwhelming odds. In most cases, supporters rise to join the cause, and the hero eventually wins the day, although in some cases, the hero might ultimately lose his life.

In the real world, of course, we don't get an advanced copy of the script, so we don't know how things will work out when we take a stand. That's what makes it so challenging to go it alone—there are no guarantees that we'll end up winning the day or converting the crowd. In fact, we probably won't.

But in one sense, we do have an advanced copy of the script—make that *the Script*. It tells us that if we stand alone for the right reasons, we won't be left alone, and our courage will be rewarded, even if it's in ways we can't fully understand. This Script tells us not to "get tired of doing good, for we will reap at the proper time if we don't give up" (Gal. 6:9). This Script also tells us we won't face a temptation that's not "common to humanity" and that God is faithful in seeing us through it. "He will not allow you to be tempted beyond what you are able, but with the temptation he will also provide a way out so that you may be able to bear it" (1 Cor. 10:13).

That doesn't mean standing alone is easy or comfortable. In fact, it almost never is. Being accepted by others is a universal desire, and you don't age out of it. Men of all ages must, on occasion, stand alone or against the current of the crowd, whether that's at work or in their community or even among friends. And while you might get better at it, it never gets easy.

In fact, there might even be occasions when you have to stand alone in a group of Christians. Peer pressure from other Christians might come in the form of a prejudice, an off-color joke, or self-righteous judgmentalism. Some Christians don't know how to embrace people who are outside their belief system, and their only response is ridicule and isolation.

Even when you know you have the support of your friends, you can rest assured that there are forces working against you. Evil people often have an agenda to drag you down, so they try to set up traps to snare you and holes for you to step in. Proverbs 1:10–15 warns against falling in with these types of pseudo-friends.

As with many virtues in life, standing alone requires preparation. If you say you'll stand up for what's right, but you haven't prepared to do it, chances are you'll never actually take that stand when it matters. And as Theodore Roosevelt once said, "Knowing what's right doesn't mean much unless you do what's right."[1]

So, how do you prepare to stand alone?

First, standing alone requires a soft heart but a firm conviction. Don't let pride and arrogance become the source of your independence. It is hard to stand alone and not be overly judgmental of others, but remember, you are no better than others or less sinful when you stand alone. The source of your stand should be your commitment to Jesus and the things He has laid down as the path of righteousness.

By keeping a soft heart toward others, you maintain a healthy understanding of your own sinfulness, a deep-seated respect for those around you, and a posture of connectedness for spiritual influence. At the same time, you must be willing and able to say, "I can't do that" or "I can't go there." You have to be willing to say something is wrong and, in some cases, to warn others that they are treading into dangerous waters. But you have to learn to stand firm without calling attention to yourself as the better person.

Second, don't wait until temptation is in full swing to decide what is right and wrong. Establish a baseline—a set of core beliefs—ahead of time and set your life against those core convictions. Without a reservoir of truth and convictions rooted in your heart and mind, you will never feel the need to stand alone. That reservoir comes from the Script: "I have treasured your word in my heart," the psalmist writes, "so that I may not sin against you" (Ps. 119:11).

Third, develop a strong muscle of security and a deep desire to please God. There are personal joy and satisfaction when we do the right thing, even if we are alone. Learning to stand alone pays deep, soul benefits. The day-after feeling is one of joy and fulfillment, not regret and disappointment and guilt—even if the stand costs you something.

This will lead you back to the first point—not to grow arrogant in taking your stand. God is always your audience and the object of your attention, and it is His approval you need, not the approval of others. But none of us have a lock on God's will. If you stand alone in everything, chances are your belief system is off base. At the extremes, this is what leads to cults and isolated nonconformists.

You are called to live in the world enough to have an audience and to have influence. But you are called to stand alone in the world enough to look different, to look like Christ, when needed. It's not your job to be the perpetual conscience of your friends or coworkers; that is the job of the Holy Spirit. It is your job to listen to the Spirit as He shapes your own convictions and conscience. This is a delicate dance for sure.

Insights to Deposit

1. Learn to stand alone when people are going places you should not go.

2. Learn to stand alone when people are saying things you should not listen to or participate in.

3. Learn to stand alone when people are acting in ways you should not act.

4. Recognize that, as a follower of Christ, even when you are standing alone in this life, you are never truly standing alone.

Questions

1. How sure are you in the core values that inform you as to when and where you should draw a line and stand alone?

2. When have you stood alone or seen someone close to you stand alone against the crowd? What did you learn from it?

3. Describe a scenario in your life where you might need to take a stand. How are you preparing now for when that day comes?

Dating Tips

*Dating should be a terrific greenhouse
for growing and learning how
to relate well to other people.*

I f you think dating is complex, confusing, and downright frustrating, then you can blame George Ade.

As a columnist for the *Chicago Record*, Ade wrote "Stories of the Streets and of the Town," a humorous series that used fictional characters to describe life in the late 1800s and early 1900s. At the time, more and more women were entering the workforce and becoming less dependent on family when it came to courtship. One of Ade's characters, a clerk named Artie, was discovering firsthand that the rules of the game were changing. When Artie realized he was losing his girl to someone else, he confronted her: "I s'pose the other boy's fillin' all my dates?" he said in a column by Ade in 1896.

With that, the world kissed dating hello, as the term entered the American vernacular.

Courtships once were heavily orchestrated by family members, and that's still the case in some cultures. But dating, especially as it has evolved over the last hundred or so years in the

West, often seems to lack an agreed-upon purpose, much less common rules for engagement. It's like walking onto a basketball court and having someone toss you badminton equipment and tell you to play hockey. You can give it a shot, but you're really just making everything up as you go.

I have heard some whacky advice about dating through the years:

> Don't spend too much time dating—it's dangerous and will be a bad influence on you.
>
> Spend tons of time dating to develop your EQ and RQ (emotional and relational intelligence).
>
> Don't date longer than a year unless you are ready to marry.
>
> Don't ever date—just find your marriage partner and get married.
>
> There should be no physical touching, handholding, hugging, or kissing before you get married.
>
> Chemistry is not that important. It is about endurance.
>
> Only date in groups of married people.
>
> Never be alone with your date.
>
> Only date people you would marry.

There might be some kernels of wisdom in a few of those, but most of it's pure bunk. Yet, learning to date in appropriate ways is vital for today's men (and women). Dating poorly yields disastrous results—emotional heartache that can leave lifelong scars. Dating well still can lead to some heartache, but the fruits also include personal growth and, in some cases, a lifelong relationship in marriage.

But every guy is different, every girl is different, and the culture is constantly changing the rules. So, what's a guy to do? Fortunately, God is never-changing and His Word provides some wise dating tips that would have helped Artie back in 1896 and that still apply today.

For instance, prioritizing your love for and pursuit of Jesus as the core driver of your life is and always has been the place to start.

When asked for the most important commandment, Jesus quoted Deuteronomy 6:4–5 and when He said, "Love the Lord your God with all your heart, with all your soul, with all your mind, and with all your strength" (Mark 12:30). Notice that He uses the word *all* as opposed to *some*. It's an all-in love for God that allows us to understand how to truly love others.

Another enduring guideline is to seek compatibility without forcing it.

Researchers have found compatibility to be the most important factor in sustaining long-term relationships, so find mutual interests and spend time, energy, and money on them.

Compatibility is the basis for friendship. For followers of Jesus, it includes the idea of being equally yoked (2 Cor. 6:14–18). But it isn't "sameness" or being a "perfect" match. It means enjoying many of the same things while having differences that complement each other in the relationship. And it means knowing the difference between a genuine willingness to sacrifice for someone and a forced sacrifice that leads to bitterness. There are times in a relationship when we do things that aren't a huge interest to us simply because we care about the other person. Maybe you take a dance class or she goes to a baseball game. But when the mutual interests aren't there, don't pretend that they are.

Relationships are dynamic, not one dimensional, so it's always important to take a holistic approach to a healthy relationship.

People are emotional, mental, physical, and spiritual. Learn your masculine role and how to operate in it. Understand her feminine role and how to respect and appreciate it. Be curious and ask deeper questions. Learn the things that matter to her and share the things that matter to you. That includes learning her "love language." Get to know her family, friends, and peers. Give each other space. Then, as the relationship endures, romance each other.

Being deliberate, however, doesn't mean you can't or shouldn't have fun and some light moments.

There are times when relationships need to be serious and intentional, but compatible couples learn how to laugh together, how to sit quietly together, how to cry together, and how to enjoy life together.

They also learn how to exit a dating relationship.

An old song points out that breaking up is hard to do. The alternative of maintaining a dating relationship for the wrong reasons, however, leads to pain. The way to end a relationship is much the same as the way to strengthen it—by putting God first and showing love and grace to the other person.

Insights to Deposit

1. The first and foremost object of our love is God, not ourselves or the person we're dating.

2. Knowing what you believe and what the other person believes is a key to knowing if you complement each other in a compatible fashion.

3. Don't be one-dimensional in your dating relationship.

4. Set clear boundaries and expectations early in the relationship, and then hold each other accountable.

Questions

1. What are the main reasons you want to date (or don't want to date)?

2. Why is it wise to avoid dating someone who doesn't share your faith beliefs? (Remember, the Bible tells us not to be "unequally yoked" to an unbeliever.)

3. What are some of the potential pitfalls of dating someone without regard for compatibility?

4. Where did you develop most of your relationship skills?

Getting Married

Marriage is a lifelong greenhouse for
personal growth and development and
can be a surprising lifeline to God.

The modern American approach to finding a spouse can look a lot like the approach to buying a car. You go somewhere with lots of options, look for something you like and think will make you happy, take a test-drive, and, provided you still think you've found a match, make your best deal. A few years later, when the paint has faded a little and there's a dent or two in the bumper, you trade for a different model.

The biblical model pretty much flips that approach on its head. For followers of Christ, a healthy marriage is all about a healthy relationship with Jesus. That leads to personal joy and a healthy relationship with your spouse. Tim Keller points out that men will never be a "good groom" to our wives if we aren't first "a good bride to Jesus."[1]

Unfortunately, the statistics tell a sad story. Marriages between professing Christians are just as likely to end in divorce as marriages between non-Christians. That's because Christians aren't immune to the pull of the cultural model for courtship and the self-centeredness in the heart of every human. We tend to lose sight of the biblical model and slip, even if unintentionally, into the Hollywood model. When it comes to finding a spouse, emotions rule, but emotions are a sandy foundation for a lasting relationship.

So, what's the recipe for success?

People write volumes on this topic, but I'll boil it down to two things I know. One, your marriage will never be all God intends for it to be if God isn't central to your story. And, two, compatibility is vital to any healthy relationship and especially in a marriage.

I was twenty-nine when Karen and I were married, so you might think waiting that long gave me some advantages when it came to maturity and preparation for what was to come. But I had no concept of what I was doing, and I proved it often in those first few years.

My parents divorced when I was young, and my dad wasn't part of my life. And even though I had some great father figures who had stepped in, I had a pretty inadequate, immature, underdeveloped understanding of what marriage really was, what a husband is really called to be. On the other hand, Karen and I had a huge advantage—we both had a vibrant walk with Jesus and we were compatible in a bunch of areas.

The value of compatibility, which I also touched on in the deposit on dating tips, really hit home for me a few years ago during a dinner in Colorado. I was at a table that included psychologist Neil Clark Warren, the founder of the eHarmony match-making site. One of the other dinner guests was fascinated by Warren's work and peppered him all evening with questions. I'm telling you, this guy saw his opportunity, took it, and got his money's worth! And while I seldom use such a setting for that type of grilling, I benefited, as well. The main thing I learned was this: research proves that compatibility is a significant key to all strong marriages.

Followers of Christ, however, too often skip over that factor because they think they've got the ultimate glue in Jesus. They say or think things like, *She says she's a Christian and I enjoy being with her, so God will fix all those annoying things about her that drive me crazy.* Or . . . *We don't know each other very well but since we both go to church it should work out.*

I'm certainly not denying or downplaying the power of God in a relationship. I'm saying that starting a marriage in a relationship that's low on compatibility is a recipe for burned bacon. I'm also not saying you have to love all the same things and think exactly alike. That's not compatibility. In marriage, the partners strengthen each other and support each other. They align on the bigger issues of life, and their personality differences complement each other.

The biggest issue of life, of course, is our view of God. Without God at the center, the most compatible couple in the world will never experience anything more than temporal worldly happiness. Compatible followers of Christ create fewer storms in their marriage. And with God at the center, they have an anchor against the strongest gale, whether they created it or it arose from circumstances beyond their control.

Psalm 127:1–2 says, "Unless the LORD builds a house, its builders labor over it in vain; unless the LORD watches over a city, the watchman stays alert in vain. In vain you get up early and stay up late, working hard to have enough food—yes, he gives sleep to the one he loves."

This isn't a text you'll hear at many weddings, but it provides a wonderful framework for marriage that's based on three key attributes of God—He is the marriage builder, the marriage protector, and the marriage transformer.

God is the marriage builder. ("Unless the LORD builds a house, its builders labor over it in vain." —Ps. 127:1a)

You play a role in the ongoing courtship, of course. There are awkward kisses under the moonlight, miles of walks in the park, and hours of deep conversations, but you need the hand of the Divine builder to construct the best that marriage has to offer.

God's blueprint is to build a unique oneness. It's been said that the goal of marriage is not to think alike but to think together. Divine oneness has a strength and beauty that are remarkable.

God also wants to build a divine greenhouse where you and your spouse grow and mature together spiritually, whatever roles you happen to be playing in life—as husband and wife, dad and mom, friends, partners, workers, volunteers. Marriage is the soil in which you can become a better, more mature version of yourself.

God is the marriage protector. ("Unless the LORD watches over a city, the watchman stays alert in vain." —Ps. 127:1b)

In the ancient cities, guards patrolled at night to watch for enemies who might attack unexpectedly. If we keep our marriage within the walls of God's city, we can count on His protection.

God is always on guard. He never sleeps, never takes a break, never gets bored, distracted, or frustrated, and never clocks out. The danger lurks when you wander off or are lured away from God's protection. Old friends, new friends, even family members have been known to pull people out. Work, hobbies, or even children can pull you out of your city (marriage).

God is the marriage transformer. ("In vain you get up early and stay up late, working hard to have enough food—yes, he gives sleep to the one he loves." —Ps. 127:2)

Why do you get up early and stay up late? To stay ahead of others and get it all done. To put in a little extra effort. There is a notion that if you just stay disciplined you can do it all on your own. You can be a self-made, self-sufficient individual. While there is some virtue to that, sometimes your best effort, discipline, intelligence, and determination comes up short. You need wisdom and strength bigger than what you have in yourself.

Eventually, you will find yourself running on empty for a season in your marriage. You need a source of strength and wisdom bigger than yourself. When you get stuck, empty of hope, and lacking optimism, you can remember that Jesus is the miracle worker.

Insights to Deposit

1. Marriage is an institution designed by God (Gen. 2:24–25 and Matt. 19:4–6).

2. Marriage is an exercise in submission—first to God and then to each other (Eph. 5:21–33).

3. Marriage is sacrifice in action. ("In sharp contrast with our culture, the Bible teaches that the essence of marriage is a sacrificial commitment to the good of the other. That means that love is more fundamentally action than emotion."[2] —Tim Keller)

Questions

1. What do sacrifice and selflessness look like in the daily lives of people who are married?

2. When you think of a great marriage, who comes to mind?

3. Why is it important to focus on becoming the right person rather than finding the right person?

4. In what areas of life is compatibility most important when building a successful marriage relationship?

5. How do compatibility and trusting God work together in a strong marriage relationship?

Building Family

*A vibrant family creates deep roots
and is a launching pad for life.*

O ur younger daughter had moved to another state and was experiencing one of those days when she longed to hear from and see the rest of her family. So, Julianne sent a group text to the rest of us and asked that we all send her a selfie.

From that request, a tradition was born. Now we have an unwritten rule in our family: When the group text comes in, we all stop what we're doing, snap a photo (which can include other people, if some are around), and send it to the group. It doesn't matter if we're having tea with the Queen of England—we make it happen.[1]

There's no set day for this family photo bomb—my phone blows up— although it typically happens on Friday mornings. And there's no set time. One week, the first text arrived very early in the day when one daughter sent a crooked head shot. Our son sent one of himself shaving in the mirror. My wife only dared to capture the top of her head and reading glasses.

Our other daughter looked like she was posing for a police lineup. And I was in my car.

These photos don't go to the world. They don't go on Facebook or Instagram. They go to the "G-5" group text account—me, my wife, and our three kids. Our family.

For many people in America, and around the world, for that matter, the word *family* is preceded mentally by an adjective: *dysfunctional*. And the reality is, no family is perfect. But family is important. And building a strong family unit is important, not only to the members of that family, but to the fabric of society. The first social institution God created was the family, when He performed the wedding ceremony of Adam and Eve. This family would be the essential unit to building society, and this is still how it works today. So, whether you are in a family with four generations of fantastic or you're from a small, broken, patched together, and somewhat whacky tribe, you have an obligation to make the most of the family you're in, now and in the future.

I have one sibling, a sister, who has passed. My mother was adopted—she had no siblings, and her adoptive parents have long since passed away. In other words, my family tree looks a bit like a fence post. My wife, on the other hand, has a huge family that's always been full of energy and love. I was immediately attracted to it. And, by the way, Karen's maiden name is Kile—the name we gave our son.

We have never lived around our full extended family, so we have developed a very tight network of friends who have supported us as family. But even with that we still directed energy and resources toward staying connected to our family. And I've never regretted any investment I've made in the health of our family.

God established the family as an institution before the fall, so there's no questioning its importance. It helps provide a sense of security, a framework for unconditional love and loyalty, a place to belong, and a greenhouse in which to grow. Family members share emotional bonds and common values. They encourage one another and contribute to one another's well-being.

Family members, of course, know us better than anyone, which means they see us at our worst and know about the baggage we hide from the rest of the world. At times, that knowledge can become a weapon; at other times, the very same knowledge is the source of empathy, forgiveness, and healing.

Perhaps the worst thing we can do is take a "whatever" approach to family. We need to champion the family. We need to work at making it work. We need to commit, early in life, to preserving and building our family, whether our family tree looks like a fence post or a banyan.

Life is hard. Family provides the love and support we need to make the most of the journey—not to mention some of the most unusual selfies the rest of the world will never see.

Insights to Deposit

1. Your role in a family can change with your season of life. Play the part God has called you to play. ("Children, obey your parents in the Lord, because this is right. Honor your father and mother, which is the first commandment with a promise, so that it may go well with you and that you may have a long life in the land. Fathers, don't stir up anger in your children, but bring them up in the training and instruction of the Lord." —Eph. 6:1–4)

2. Learn to ask, give, and practice forgiveness. Love covers a multitude of sins. ("For if you forgive others their offenses, your heavenly Father will forgive you as well." —Matt. 6:14)

3. Become a champion of family. ("But if anyone does not provide for his own family, especially for his own household, he has denied the faith and is worse than an unbeliever." —1 Tim. 5:8)

4. Initiate love, interest, and communication with your family members, regardless of how they respond. Someone has to be the first mover. Make that you.

Questions

1. What family traditions mean the most to you?

2. Describe your family—what you love most about it, what you see as weird or strange, what you'd like to see changed.

3. What characteristics and qualities do you envision for the family you might someday start?

4. How can the dysfunctions of your family serve as a means for you to love and empathize with them, rather than judge them?

PART 5

My Work

*A musician must make his music,
an artist must paint, a poet must
write if he is to ultimately be
at peace with himself.*[1]
—Abraham Maslow

Taking Initiative

Initiative is obedience in action
regardless of the risks.

I once was a partner in a start-up called The Life@Work Company. It was founded on the simple idea of trying to catalyze a movement around the intersection of faith and work. After repeated, unsuccessful attempts to get other national organizations to lead the charge, my business partner and I finally embraced the reality that it was our calling.

An angel investor had come out of nowhere and pledged as much money as needed to get the company off the ground. So, off we went.

Central to our strategy was a magazine that explored how to combine biblical wisdom and business excellence. It was a huge success. Everywhere we went, people talked about the magazine. Subscribers were signing up faster than we could assimilate them.

While we were sailing full-speed toward a land well beyond our expectations, we were constantly juggling the right structure to unleash the movement. We even changed our formal structure from for profit to nonprofit and back. By the summer of 2001, we felt that we had it all packaged correctly. A private equity firm in Chicago agreed to put big money into the brand. We struck a deal and the sky was the limit. We moved the headquarters to Nashville and hired a world-class publisher. We were rolling.

Then that horrible national disaster called 9/11 happened. It took a couple of months, but the fear and panic in our country caused an economic meltdown in some circles. By the time we realized our private equity partner was going under, it was too late.

Someone in our company had to take initiative and figure out a path forward. We were at a crossroads, and the quicksand in that intersection was pulling us all down. We all were in shock and in despair because of the money we had lost. It was paralyzing for some, and it fell to me to take whatever actions we would take to recover.

I spent almost fifteen solid months focused, head down, in an effort to lead the company out of ruin and save the brand. We met with every single investor, looked them in their eyes, and told them the story. We negotiated millions in obligations and sold the company to keep everyone whole. I didn't do it all by myself, but I did play the role of emotional and directional leader. And, in retrospect, the lessons I had learned from my mother about initiative and courage saved something far more important than a company—those lessons saved my reputation.

Initiative, at its core, is taking the early steps of obedience to what we know God is calling us to do. Knowing what God is calling us to do comes from a strong connection to God by reading His word and communicating in prayer. Inevitably, that calling takes us out of our comfort zone because it involves risks and requires faith.

On our best days, we are like Peter when he stepped out of the boat and walked toward Jesus. On our worst days, we are like Peter when he took his eyes off Christ, realized he was walking across water, and sank like a rock until his Savior rescued him from sleeping with the fish.

Initiative is a character trait that we develop over time by strengthening our faith and acting in obedience over and over and over until our first and enduring instinct is to take action and trust God for the results.

Jesus was teaching in a village one day when some men brought their paralytic friend in hopes that Jesus would heal him. When they arrived, however, the crowd was so large that there was no way to get in the house where Jesus was teaching, much less to ask for His help. But they knew Jesus was the answer, so they found a way. They went on the roof, dug a hole through it, and lowered their friend to the feet of Jesus.

Pause a second and imagine that scene!

These guys were desperate. These guys had faith. And, so, these guys took the risky initiative that led to a miracle healing and, even more importantly, to the forgiveness of sins. In fact, the first thing Jesus did was commend their faith. "Seeing their faith he said, 'Friend, your sins are forgiven'" (Luke 5:20). When the Pharisees questioned His authority to forgive sins, that's when Jesus healed the paralytic.

When we take initiative out of obedience to God and trust Him for the rest, the results might not look like we expected, but they always work for our good.

Insights to Deposit

1. Initiative is as much a character trait as it is a personality trait.

2. Never wait or rationalize initiative away. Take a step. If you know it's the right thing to do, push yourself into an action then let your brain and emotions catch up if necessary.

3. Initiative often takes faith, because we are unsure how things will turn out. Without risk, we seldom try anything new. Initiative and risk go hand in hand.

Questions

1. React to this statement: "Some people watch things happen. Some people make things happen. Some people wonder what happened." Which best describes you?

2. How important is initiative for a man when it comes to dating, making friends, and working?

3. What role does initiative play in communication, asking forgiveness, giving grace, extending a helping hand, offering encouragement or advice, and making decisions?

4. How do you balance taking human initiative and waiting on God?

Setting Goals

Paint God-centered goals on your heart, and
they will guide you toward your dreams.

I knew from a pretty young age that I wanted to go to college, earn a Master's degree, and maybe even pursue a doctorate. Why? Because I felt it was good stewardship of my gifts, a great gift back to my mom, and that it would increase my chances of landing and excelling at good work.

That might seem like pretty standard stuff for some folks in America, but nothing along those lines was assumed for me. I didn't grow up in a professional family where the kids automatically followed their parents to their college of tradition. Instead, it was up to me to paint those goals on my heart and go to work making them happen.

It wasn't always easy. I had setbacks and things didn't always go as planned, so I had to make constant adjustments. It took me a few more years to complete my formal education than it did for some folks, partly because I sometimes needed my bank account to catch up with my educational ambitions and partly because my curiosity took me down a few rabbit trails. Those detours were incredibly educational, but not really efficient for someone trying to grab a degree and get out quick. Eventually, however, I completed my formal classroom education.

Goal: Earn a Master's and a doctorate degree. Check!

Another goal I set early on was to figure out my unique calling and be in that career zone by the time I turned thirty-five. This turned out to be much tougher than moving through the halls of academia. But, I stayed with it and kept pushing forward, even when I was hit by a bit of confusion or a bump in the road.

Did I make it? You bet.

Beat that one by a couple of years. Check!

Just because we come up with a goal doesn't mean it should happen or that it will happen. We know that. On the other hand, setting goals is a practical part of navigating life. As the legendary baseball coach and philosopher Yogi Berra put it, "If you don't know where you're going, you might not get there."[1] And one unknown wit warned that "in the absence of clearly defined goals, we become strangely loyal to performing daily acts of trivia."

Putting specifics (language and dates) to our innermost desires can be a very powerful habit. It can truly act as the North Star that guides us during dark nights, through tough weather, or during times in life when we have so much noise and so many options that we just get a brain freeze. Author Brian Tracy called goals the "fuel in the furnace of achievement."[2]

Jesus told us not to worry about life—about what we will eat or drink, about the clothes we will wear, or about our future (see Matt. 6:25–34). But He wasn't saying it's wrong to set goals. When He talked about the high cost of being His disciple, in fact, He used planning as an analogy. "Suppose one of you wants to build a tower," He said. "Won't you first sit down and estimate the cost to see if you have enough money to complete it?" (Luke 14:28 NIV). Likewise, Habakkuk advises us to "Write the vision; make it plain, so that the one who reads it can run toward it" (Hab. 2:2).

Scripture, in fact, talks a good bit about the value of setting goals and planning for the future, but there's an important caveat: The goals and plans have to be God-centered, not me-centered. Proverbs 16:9 tells us, "We can make our plans, but the LORD determines our steps." The apostle James points out that we don't know what will happen tomorrow and that our lives are but a mist, so we should say, "If the Lord wills, we will live and do this or that" (James 4:15). And Jesus tells us in that Matthew passage I referenced earlier that if we "seek first his kingdom and his righteousness," God will take care of our needs (Matt. 6:33).

Every year, I review the year behind and ponder and pray about the year ahead. Then I set goals in most areas of my life. I have done this since my first years in college, and few things have helped steer my life better.

Goal-setting is a discipline, not a magic trick. Magic is mystifying and tricky. And nothing really changes . . . it just looks like it does. Applying a discipline is hard, but it's available to anyone willing to enroll in the program and do the work. And best of all, things really can and do change. Tomorrow can be different than yesterday. Goal-setting can make that happen.

Insights to Deposit

1. A goal needs to be honorable, personal, attainable, and measurable.

2. It is important to balance two principles in goal-setting: One: don't be shallow and impulsive in the pursuit of your vision, dream, or goal. And two: don't be presumptive and arrogant about yourself.

3. Wrapping your heart around a goal and taking a risk can be very powerful.

4. No goal is too small or too big if it is part of God's plan for you.

Questions

1. Name one goal you have set and achieved.

2. What's the difference between wishing, dreaming, and goal-setting?

3. Why is goal-setting easier for some personality types than others? What types find it easier? Or harder?

Working Hard

*Some things are accomplished only by
exerting muscle power and brain cells.*

---

ertain stretches in life seem to be straight uphill. In other
words, sometimes life is harder than other times.

I know that has been true for me.

I remember working two jobs all the way through college
so I could pay for my tuition and other expenses. I remember
the years when I was working full time, newly married, and
finishing my doctoral degree. And I remember when a partner
and I launched our initial company and seemed to be working
around the clock for almost a year. I would work all day, come
home and spend time with my wife until she went to bed, and
then work until 2 a.m. Then I'd do it all over the next day.

That doesn't make me special or different. It makes me . . .
normal.

Sometimes life is just hard, and not just for adults. In fact,
as I write this chapter, I've been noticing a good bit of news
coverage lately about the increasingly high rates of depression
among teenagers. Expectations are high and the competition
is stiff.

When Kile was a sophomore in high school, one of the areas where he faced an uphill battle was on the basketball court. He made the varsity squad, which was great news, but keeping up with his peers was no easy task. The team was undefeated state champions and ranked No. 8 in the nation the previous year, and it returned two of the top players in the state—players Kile would have to guard and be guarded by every day in practice.

He came home many days worn out, not just physically but emotionally.

Life is hard, but those hard days yielded some fantastic results. Kile learned great lessons about persistence, he improved his skills as a basketball player (mentally and physically), and he contributed for the next three years on teams that were extremely successful.

Yes, life is often hard. But there is value in the hard things of life.

Babe Ruth, the legendary baseball player, once pointed out that, "You just can't beat the person who never gives up."[1] But staying in the fight is just one aspect of the battle. I've learned, from my experiences and from studying others, that former General Colin Powell was right on point when he said success is "the result of preparation, hard work, and learning from failure."[2] In other words, it's the result of making the most of those inevitable hard times in life.

One of the best breakdowns of this reality is found in 2 Timothy 2:3–6.

"Share in suffering like a good soldier of Christ Jesus," Paul writes. "No one serving as a soldier gets entangled in the concerns of civilian life; he seeks to please the commanding officer. Also, if anyone competes as an athlete, he is not crowned unless he competes according to the rules. The hardworking farmer ought be the first to get a share of the crops."

Paul says we should approach life as a soldier, an athlete, and a farmer. All are pictures of men doing something hard.

- Endure like the soldier–A "good job" from the commanding officer awaits the soldier who stays focused and committed to his orders. He has been off fighting wars and enduring extreme hours of hardship. He then comes home, and his commanding officer stops him and says, "Good job, son."
- Compete like the athlete–A crown awaits the athlete who is off by himself working on his game. All his buddies are partying and wasting time. They chose the easy path. But then the day of the big game comes. His buddies are all in the stands, and the athlete who has been working hard comes out. He competes and wins. Internally, he feels a deep sense of accomplishment that only comes through a hard-fought competition.
- Persist like the farmer—A harvest awaits the farmer after getting up early in the dark and working all day in the hot summer sun. His hours are long and the work is extremely painful. But, the fall eventually arrives and he has a harvest. That is his reward for his work. He has enough food to feed his family and can even sell some or

give some to others in need. His endurance
has paid off.

Insights to Deposit

1. Hard is supposed to be hard work. Endure like the soldier, compete like the athlete, and persist like the farmer.

2. Hard work requires support from God and others. Because hard work isn't easy, Paul offered some words of encouragement for weary workers in his letter to the Galatians. "Let us not get tired of doing good, for we will reap at the proper time if we don't give up" (Gal. 6:9).

3. God sees it all and does not turn a blind eye to your effort.

Questions

1. What is hard about your current season in life?

2. What does working hard look like? Is it more about number of hours, putting your heart into it, or persistence?

3. What rewards would you like to see for persevering and working hard?

4. How do you persevere when you work hard but don't see the results you'd like to see?

5. What promise do you cling to from God about working hard?

Handling Money

Hold money loosely and share it liberally.

My mom and my mentors taught me some practical lessons during my formative years about handling money, and I studied the topic in college, both in business classes and in theology classes. I also learned from some real-word experiences as a young adult. But few things shaped my view of money like an impromptu experience with a friend in 1986.

We'd gotten to know each other at church not long after my wife and I moved to Fayetteville, Arkansas, and he called me early one evening during the week leading up to Christmas.

"You want to do something fun?" he said.

"Sure," I said. "What's up?"

"Meet me in thirty minutes," he said. "We're gonna make some Christmas deliveries around town."

I thought we were going to hand out some homemade cookies or gift cards. When we got together, however, I discovered that he had taken his entire Christmas bonus—thousands of dollars—and stuffed it in a bunch of white envelopes. The envelopes weren't addressed to anyone, nor did they include any type of note. They were just plain, white envelopes, ordinary in every sense—except for the hundred-dollar bills inside them. Then we spend two hours driving around town and putting those envelops in the mailboxes of people he had identified as having a financial need—everyone from a single mom shouldering the full load of raising four kids to an aging couple hanging on by a thread.

It was his bonus. He wasn't taking money out of his company. He was taking something he had earned, and, after prayer and agreement with his wife, giving it to people who were less fortunate. He wasn't doing it to earn their praise or their respect. He was doing it out of compassion and obedience—because he felt called to do it. And, what's more, he did it every year.

My first question: *Is this dumb?*

My second question: *Is this safe?*

Later, the questions grew deeper.

For the first time, I found myself wrestling with what it *really* means to hold money loosely and share it liberally. I had to explore the dark side of my heart and money. Before that, my mind-set about money was partly practical and partly theoretical. But when I found myself pulled into his narrative, I had to confront how my stated views aligned with the way I was earning, spending, investing, and sharing money.

You could make the case that my friend didn't need what probably amounted to around $10,000. But I don't know anybody who doesn't have a use for $10,000. This guy was wealthy, but he also had learned the lesson of handling money correctly. And his example challenged me to figure out what it meant for me and the way I handled money. Was money my idol, something I worshiped without realizing it? Or was I managing it faithfully and responsibly? And, more importantly, was I willing to let it go as easily as my friend?

It's easy to talk a good game when it comes to money, but harder to live up to our words. Thomas Jefferson famously advised his granddaughter, "Never spend your money before you have it."[1] But he was notorious for going heavily into debt, in part because of extravagant luxury purchases. And while he kept meticulous records of his spending, there's no evidence that he ever actually balanced his books. At his death, Jefferson's debts totaled $107,000—well over $1 million in today's economy, and his family had to sell much of his property, including his beloved home, Monticello, to settle his accounts.

Jefferson, like so many of us, knew how to handle money *in theory*, but didn't handle it very well *in practice*. How about you?

My personal approach to handling money well rests on five guiding principles:

> **Earn it honestly . . .** ("Opportunity is missed by most people because it is dressed in overalls and looks like work."[2] —Anonymous)
>
> **Spend it carefully . . .** ("We buy things we don't need with money we don't have to impress people we don't like."[3] —Dave Ramsey)
>
> **Invest it thoughtfully . . .** ("Do not store up for yourselves treasures on earth, where moth and rust destroy, and where thieves break in and steal. But store up for yourselves treasures in heaven, where moth and rust do not destroy, and where thieves do not break in and steal. For where your treasure is, there your heart will be also." —Jesus, Matt. 6:19–21)

Share it liberally . . . ("Money is like muck, not good except it be spread."[4] —Francis Bacon)

Hold it loosely . . . ("When you chase money, you're going to lose. You're just going to. Even if you get the money, you're not going to be happy."[5] —Gary Vaynerchuk)

Insights to Deposit

1. Money, like all your possessions, belongs to God (Ps. 50:8–12).

2. The love of money, not money itself, is the root of all kinds of evil. Therefore, the way you handle money demonstrates where your heart and your faith truly rest.

3. God blesses you financially so you can bless others. Therefore, money can be a powerful tool in the hands of a mature person of faith.

4. Money can't make you but it can certainly ruin you . . . ("The little that the righteous person has is better than the abundance of many wicked people. For the arms of the wicked will be broken, but the LORD supports the righteous." —Ps. 37:16–17)

Questions

1. Who is the *poorest rich person* you know?

2. Who is the *richest poor person* you know?

3. What would you do with $100,000 if it were in your bank account?

4. How does the way Jesus call you to handle your money distinguish you from the rest of the world?

Having Ambition

You should aspire to do good, have a positive impact, and reach your potential.

A mbition is a concept loaded with meaning but starving for clarity. It has been abused, neglected, misunderstood, and misappropriated for years. And it's an especially confusing topic these days for young men who are followers of Jesus.

The common myths will tell you that ambition is an underlying destructive force for Christians because it feeds on our selfishness and greed. God calls us to meekness and humility, after all, and those qualities run counter to ambition, do they not?

Well, not really. Ambition is simply a strong motivation to achieve something. The real antonyms for ambition are indifference, apathy, and laziness—not godly qualities at all. The more relevant question around ambition shouldn't be whether ambition is a good thing but whether the focus of our ambition is on good things and lived out in godly ways. So, when Kile and I discussed this topic, we started with a short survey about ambition. Here it is, if you'd like to take it:

Score each of the following as good, bad, or neutral ambition:

- Desiring to be the president of a pro sports team
- Desiring to discover the cure for cancer
- Desiring to play college sports
- Desiring to date a really great looking gal
- Desiring to graduate top in the class or get a college scholarship
- Desiring to make a lot of money
- Desiring to reverse the trend in homelessness and poverty
- Desiring to be a CEO
- Desiring to own a company
- Desiring to get a Master's degree and/or a PhD
- Desiring to lead a church that impacts an entire city

We have all different types of ambitions. Some are worthy and some are not. Ambition in and of itself is neither good nor bad. It only gains moral weight as a result of what we attach it to and why we attach it. Consider the words that regularly ride along with ambition—words like *build, acquire, pursue, rule, expand, compete,* and *multiply.* Depending on what we attach to these words, they may indicate something admirable or something loathsome. Ultimately, each of us is in control of what we attach to our ambition.

Nothing I find in Scripture indicates that God wants to strip us of our ambition; rather, He wants to strip us of our *selfish* ambition. The apostle Paul, for instance, experienced a radical transformation on the road to Damascus, but what we often miss is that much of Paul did not change. He was an aggressive, independent, get-it-done kind of guy before his transformation, and he was still that guy afterward. What changed were his heart and the target of his drive. God didn't destroy Paul's ambition; God redeemed his ambition and harnessed it for good. Likewise, He wants to strap your ambition (and mine) to the gospel of grace and let it drip like a rich coffee brewed daily in your life.

When ambition is filtered by a good motive, rooted in a useful outcome, and linked with the Lord's eternal plan, it becomes profoundly powerful.

Unfortunately, there is no one-size-fits-all blueprint for God-centered ambitions. They can be highly personalized or they can be shared with others. They can be tied to career, ministry, or family. They can be focused on obviously good endeavors or to the seemingly mundane tasks of life.

Regardless of the shape and size, the shared trait of God-centered ambitions is God. He leads us to the ambition and empowers us to chase it. Sure, God-centered ambition doesn't often equate to the easy living we may desire, but it offers a peace that will always elude us when we are compelled by self-centered ambition.

Insights to Deposit

1. Ambition is an inherent quality, given to all in some measure. We all don't get the same dose of inner drive, but we all get a dose. Regardless of what we do with it, ambition is something God deposits into us from birth.

2. Ambition can be rooted in self or God. The story of Solomon provides a great case study. Solomon was a man of unparalleled wisdom, and yet throughout his life he regularly swung back and forth between good and bad ambition. For Solomon and for us, the initial distinguisher when evaluating ambition should be our motives and heart.

3. Self-serving ambitions leave us empty, stuck, or full of regret.

4. God-centered ambitions are flourishing, productive, and fulfilling. Nothing is more satisfying than living out a God-centered ambition.

Questions

1. Do you think you have enough ambition?

2. Do you think your ambition is God-centered or self-centered?

3. What are your ambitions for life?

4. What makes your ambitions for life healthy?

5. What threatens to make them destructive?

Finding Your Calling

*Your calling is the sweet spot where
your work takes place, at the intersection
of your talents and passions.*

The nightmare question for many teenagers and young adults goes something like this: "What are you planning to do with your life?" And for far too many people, that question never really goes away. They might go to college, earn a degree, and spend years advancing along a career path, but the question keeps gnawing at their gut like one too many habañero peppers.

I don't know many people who haven't at one time or another wrestled with finding their calling—the sweet spot where their work takes place at the intersection of their talents and passions.

For some, understanding their passions and identifying their talents come quickly and easily. For others, it's more elusive. I have always had so many different interests that I realized early on it might take me some time to discover my zone. Sometime in my twenties, in fact, I set a goal to be in my calling and career by the time I was thirty-five. I beat that goal by a couple of years, but I realize it took me much longer than some and not nearly as long as others.

For me, it came together when a friend and I began working on a business partnership. We wanted to design our own company straight out of our strengths and passions. The talents I identified for myself: content developer, encourager, macro strategist, teacher, connector. And while that company no longer exists in its original form, I've been passionately applying those talents in my work now for more than twenty-five years. When I came to grips with who I am, it became much easier to pursue work that reflects who I am. Passion and skills began to overlap.

I believe you always should be looking for that overlap, but you shouldn't stress yourself out trying to figure out everything too quickly. Let it come to you as you journey with God every day. And remember that God might have several assignments for you during your life. Nehemiah experienced different callings and careers. They were similar in the skillset required, but they were different assignments. So, while God can call you to a number of different work assignments, more times than not they will involve your core skills, talents, and passions.

We identify our skills and talents in a number of ways. We can take assessments, lean into our experiences, and talk through them with friends and mentors. It's not always easy, because sometimes it's hard to tell something we enjoy at the moment from something that we will love for a lifetime.

Richard Bolles, who wrote the all-time best-selling book for career guidance *(What Color Is My Parachute?)*, once told a colleague of mine that your work might not always be fun but it shouldn't be devoid of love. "There is something wrong with the definition, if one ever comes to it, of saying, 'I'm doing this for God, but I hate it,'"[1] said Bolles, who started out in chemical engineering before becoming an Episcopal priest and then a career counselor and author. He went on to say that finding your sweet spot begins with something that's often overlooked in many career searches—gratitude. First, gratitude for being alive, then for the sense that God loves us enough to make us unique, and then for the fact that we, therefore, can do work that's uniquely ours. That gratitude leads to joy in our calling.

"When I see somebody who really feels called to their work," he said, "they get joy out of their work. It doesn't mean there are not stretches when they are tediously plodding through the day. But, basically, they get up alive and excited about what they are doing. They have some sense that there is something unique they have to contribute to this world. This makes them very excited."[2]

So, what about the big elephant-in-the-room question: How do we identify God's calling for our work? Scripture reveals a few different ways.

One, *God calls us directly.* He might call us by name as He did with Moses (Exod. 3:1–10), or He might directly reveal what our work will look like as He did with Paul (Acts 9:4–6).

Two, *God places a desire in our heart*—a feeling of deep responsibility to accomplish a task or meet a need (Isaiah 6; Nehemiah 1).

Three, *God arranges our path.* Josiah (2 Kings 22) followed a path because he had no other options. John the Baptist (Mark 1:2–7) followed a path that was prearranged for him.

Regardless of what the specific vocational call looks like on our lives, there is one general gospel call of God that all people share: to believe in Jesus and follow Him in a life of discipleship. As we do that and walk in faith, He will place us where we need to be.

Insights to Deposit

1. There are two kinds of calling: God calls us to salvation and God calls us to specific work assignments. (Rom. 8:28; Jer. 1:5). God's call regarding salvation is the same for every human. God's call regarding our career is unique.

2. Resist the sacred/secular split—the myth that secular vocations are bad or inferior while church or spiritual vocations are superior. As Martin Luther pointed out, "All works are measured before God by faith alone."[3]

3. Living and working in God's calling yields energy, fulfillment, and excellence, and it reflects God's glory. Being out of God's calling yields frustration, regret, turmoil, and emptiness.

4. Remember that it is never "too late" to be obedient to God's call. Don't believe the myth that you can make some decision that will unalterably remove you from the path of His will. You can always begin to obey Him, and when you do, He will use even the time you spend running from Him to shape your unique call.

Questions

1. Do you think God cares about your work and career? Why or why not?

2. What are the advantages of finding your calling and vocation and the consequences of not finding it?

3. What role do education, money, and training have in finding your calling and career?

4. Name all of the different jobs or careers you can think of that are listed in the Bible.

PART 6

My Future

*One of the ways you will know
you are on the path to God's
purpose for your life is that you will
be required to place your trust in
God in order to take the next step.*[1]

—Tony Evans

Defining Success

*If you embrace a wrong definition of success,
you will forever be climbing the wrong ladder
leaning against the wrong building.*

It's easy to say that true success isn't about acquiring more and more things—especially after you've done well financially and acquired all the things you need and most of the things you want.

I was fortunate, however, to learn that lesson early in life—way back when I was growing up as a pretty poor kid on the Mississippi Gulf Coast. One memorable year in particular shaped my early thinking about success.

That was the year when I saw a guy in high school get a sporty new Mustang for his sixteenth birthday. And that was the year my mother basically took a bunch of old Christmas cards people had given her and turned them into my single Christmas present.

Christmas cards as a Christmas present?

It was all she had.

She cut out the pictures and made a small storybook album, then presented me the gift of wisdom and encouragement in place of stuff.

I will never forget it.

I remember sitting next to our very pitiful tree and looking at my one and only present. She apologized and told me to open it, then just sat quietly as I read it. Sure, I was disappointed for a moment. But the more I read, the more the Spirit of God worked in the heart of a young teenage boy and made one huge deposit after the next into my soul. It was stuff money couldn't buy:

- It was a sense that I was deeply loved and that nothing could ever make me feel insecure.
- It was gratitude for my mom's tenacity, character, and commitment to me and my sister.
- It was a bridge of dependency upon the God of the universe to be my "daddy," even though I didn't have an earthly one.
- It was recognition that God had a plan for me, and that I was not on my own trying to figure out this thing called life.

That gift has paid more dividends than a thousand shares of Apple stock, because it helped shape my definition of success. And as I grew older, I refined my definition of success by reflecting on that gift in light of the truth of God's Word.

I realized, for instance, that my success is tied to my understanding of God's Word. Joshua 1:8 says, "This book of the law shall not depart from your mouth, but you shall meditate on it day and night, so that you may be careful to do according to all that is written in it; for then you will make your way prosperous, and then you will have success" (NASB).

We face daily pressures, as teenagers and as adults, to define our success based on what others around us think. But that's not the measure God uses. In fact, the book of Psalms opens with this reality:

> How happy is the one who does not walk in the advice of the wicked or stand in the pathway of sinners or sit in the company of mockers! Instead, his delight is in the LORD's instruction, and he meditates on it day and night. He is like a tree planted beside flowing streams that bears its fruit in its season and whose leaf does not wither. Whatever he does prospers. (Ps: 1:1–3)

This version of success is unique because it gives credit to God for everything that is good. Success isn't something I achieve, but something God achieves through me and others.

God issued a clear warning through the prophet Jeremiah about taking credit for success:

> This is what the LORD says: "The wise person should not boast in his wisdom; the strong should not boast in his strength; the wealthy should not boast in his wealth. But the one who boasts should boast in this: that he understands and knows me—that I am the LORD, showing faithful love, justice and righteousness on the earth, for I delight in these things." This is the LORD's declaration. (Jer. 9:23–24)

We're responsible for our obedience to God, but we can rest assured that any success that comes in life is the result of

His grace, not our superior intellect, planning, vision, or business savvy.

James, the half-brother of Jesus, saw no value in saying, "Today or tomorrow we will travel to such and such a city and spend a year there and do business and make a profit" (James 4:13). Why? Because we don't know what will happen tomorrow! Only God knows.

"Yet you do not know what tomorrow will bring—what your life will be!" James said. "For you are like vapor that appears for a little while, then vanishes. Instead, you should say, 'If the Lord wills, we will live and do this or that'" (vv. 14–15).

Those verses create a view of success that Erwin Lutzer, the former pastor of The Moody Church in Chicago, summarized in a way that rings true.

> "Better to love God and die unknown than to love the world and be a hero," Lutzer said. "Better to be content with poverty than die a slave to wealth; better to have taken some risks . . . and lost some battles than to have retreated from the war. . . . What a tragedy to climb the ladder of success, only to find that the ladder was leaning against the wrong wall!"[1]

Insights to Deposit

1. Success is discovering God's unique purposes for your life, and then engineering your life in that direction. ("God has not called me to be successful, He has called me to be faithful."[2] —Mother Teresa of Calcutta)

2. Success is more about who you are than what you achieve or what you stockpile. ("A strong name is better than riches." —Prov. 22:1)

3. Success touches every aspect of your life—your work, relationships, ambition, etc.—not just the spiritual dimension.

Questions

1. How would you define success?

2. How do you know when you achieve it?

3. Why are there different definitions of success for different people?

4. What difference does it make if you believe one thing versus another regarding success?

Thinking Ahead

Looking beyond the day-to-day allows
you to sort, sift, and sequence
the important things of life.

The percentage of high school seniors in the United States who have a driver's license has steadily been on the decline, dropping to around 71 percent in 2015. Many teenagers apparently feel so connected online to their friends that they see little need to hit the roads together. Plus, if they need a ride, they can just ask Mom, Dad, or one of the ride-sharing companies like Lyft or Uber.[1]

For my children, however, learning to drive and earning that license were still very much rites of passage along the road of independence. And, like most parents who have handled the duties, I'll never forget teaching our three how to drive.

They all had their ups and downs, but one in particular struggled with the idea of looking right in front of them and glancing down the road to the things ahead. It was especially challenging at night, when they literally wanted to stay focused on the area right in front of the headlights. That's not a bad place to monitor, of course, but you also want to be ready for what's coming up, not just for what's happening where you are.

Mountain bikers and motorcycle riders use the phrase "looking through the turn" to describe the important idea of simultaneously driving in the present while looking toward the future. And it's equally important as a life skill.

This idea of thinking ahead (or around corners) comes more naturally to some than to others. Personally, I'm a list guy and I always have been. Every Sunday night since I was a teenager, I've spent a few minutes looking down the road, scanning the next few weeks to see what's coming, and making my list of things to do. I love checking things off my list. You might be more intuitive and serendipitous. But even if it doesn't come naturally, thinking ahead is important. It allows you to sort, sift, and sequence the important things of life.

If it's not part of your wiring, then it's something you'll value if you develop it, because life comes with sequences. Proverbs 24:27 advises us to "complete your outdoor work, and prepare your field; afterward, build your house." And as the old saying goes, if you only have an hour to chop down a tree, spend the first forty-five minutes sharpening your ax.

This doesn't mean you have to have a well-organized sock drawer or a hundred-year plan like some corporations, but you can't always wait to the last minute to make decisions and expect success in life. You've got to look beyond the headlights that are right in front of your car.

Why?

Thinking ahead allows you to gather resources, store them, and have them available when the need arises. Proverbs 30:24–25 says, "Four things on earth are small, yet they are extremely wise: ants are not a strong people, yet they store up their food in the summer." When you think ahead and properly order the sequences of life, you'll have a better idea of where you're going, how you'll get there, and what you'll end up with when you arrive.

The danger for the planners of the world is that thinking ahead can become an issue of control. *Who does all this thinking? . . . Me! Who does this planning? . . . Me! Who is in control? . . . Me!* That type of thinking ahead puts you on the road to perdition because the thinking and planning weren't submitted to the Lord.

Even Jesus submitted His plans to the Father. "I can do nothing on my own," He said. "I judge only as I hear, and my judgment is just, because I do not seek my own will, but the will of him who sent me" (John 5:30).

As you think ahead about the sequences of life, begin with prayer, end with prayer, and trust God for the results.

Insights to Deposit

1. Thinking ahead requires us to stop our activities and gaze down the road.

2. Learn to live in the present while thinking ahead to the future.

3. Always surrender your plans to God. Remember, God isn't a consultant who hands out wise advice that you can accept or reject. He is Lord.

4. It is usually good to find a time slot every week to do this kind of thinking.

Questions

1. Does thinking ahead come naturally to you or is it something of a challenge?

2. When and where are you most comfortable thinking about the future?

3. Who helps you process what you're thinking about the future?

4. What are five things you can logically anticipate happening in your life within the next week? How can you best prepare for those events?

Making Decisions

*The decisions we make today determine the
life we'll have tomorrow.*

My wife and I have a general understanding about how we pick the restaurant when we go out for dinner: We each throw a couple of options on the table and whittle it down from there. If either has a real hunger for some local favorite, then that person gets to choose. It makes dinner-related decision-making pretty simple.

In other areas of my life, however, I can't escape the reality that almost every moment comes with some sort of decision that I must make. Some are trivial *(Should I have seconds on the catfish?)* and others are monumental *(Should I take this new client or hire this person versus that person?)*. Most fall somewhere in between. Regardless, our lives are a massive accumulation of decisions, and we all live with the consequences of our choices. That's why it's so important to learn how to make good decisions.

The life of Moses teaches us something fascinating about decision-making, and it's conveniently summarized in Hebrews 11:24–28. These five verses identify six kinds of decisions Moses made and that we are often called to make.

1. The choice of *refusal*—"By faith Moses, when he had grown up, refused to be called the son of Pharaoh's daughter" (Heb. 11:24). Moses learned to say no when the choice was wrong.

2. The choice of *acceptance*—"[He] chose to suffer with the people of God rather than to enjoy the fleeting pleasure of sin" (Heb. 11:25). Moses learned to say yes when the choice was right.

3. The choice of *contemplation*—"He considered reproach for the sake of Christ to be greater wealth than the treasures of Egypt, since he was looking ahead to the reward" (Heb. 11:26). Moses learned to assess correctly by contemplating and pondering his options when the choice was unclear.

4. The choice of *departure*—"By faith he left Egypt behind, not being afraid of the king's anger . . ." (Heb. 11:27a). Moses learned to say goodbye when the end had come.

5. The choice of *persistence*—". . . Moses persevered as one who sees him who is invisible" (Heb. 11:27b). Moses learned to hang on when the load was heavy.

6. The choice of *initiative*—"By faith he instituted the Passover and the sprinkling of the blood, so that the destroyer of the firstborn might not touch the Israelites" (Heb. 11:28). Moses learned to launch something new when there was a need.

Six kinds of decisions. Every day we dance around and between some combination of the six. The recurring thread in all of those types of decisions, of course, is found in two words: by faith.

Moses often bore the responsibility not only for his actions but for the collective direction of the people of Israel. I imagine he felt pretty lonely at times, given the weight of those responsibilities. But, clearly, he learned that he wasn't making decisions on his own. He was leaning into the wisdom of God.

Scripture tells us to seek insights and advice from advisers we can trust—other godly men and women—when we're making decisions. "Plans fail when there is no counsel," we're told in Proverbs 15:22, "but with many advisers they succeed." That counsel, however, has to be filtered through the wisdom that comes only from God (James 1:15) by submitting to God and trusting Him for the results. That's the promise of Proverbs 3:5–6: "Trust in the LORD with all your heart, and do not rely on your own understanding; in all your ways know him, and he will make your paths straight."

Insights to Deposit

1. Some people are naturally good at decision-making, while others struggle with it.

2. Every decision eventually triggers actions. A decision that isn't followed with actions is the same as making no decision. L. G. Elliott, a Canadian nuclear physicist, pointed out, "Vacillating people seldom succeed. Successful men and women are very careful in reaching their decisions, and very persistent and determined in action thereafter."[1]

3. Avoiding a decision is a decision itself. It involves consciously concluding not to decide, and then executing on that by doing nothing.

4. Our decisions expose us because they are driven by the things we truly believe and desire, whether our fears and insecurities, our pride, values, or our faith. Roy Disney once said, "It's not hard to make decisions when you know what your values are."[2]

Questions

1. Is good decision-making something that can be learned? Why or why not?

2. What role do convictions and values play in sound decision-making?

3. How does the old adage "practice makes perfect" apply to good decision-making?

4. What role does prayer play, and how does that translate into still having to pull the trigger?

Enduring Failure

Failure is an opportunity to learn
from and cling to God.

---

watched an online video recently of the final out in a Minnesota high school state tournament baseball game. Maybe you saw it, too. Every news organization from *USA Today* to NPR posted it, and it was all over social media.

There were multiple videos from all different angles, but they all showed the same thing: With his team up 4–0 and one out away from a trip to the state title game, the pitcher fires a dart for strike three. The game is over. His teammates rush toward the mound to celebrate, and the pitcher runs toward his catcher.

But then he does something totally unexpected. After a brief hug with the catcher, he breaks free and continues to home plate, where he takes the dejected batter into his arms and hugs him tightly for about ten seconds.

The pitcher and the opposing batter, it turns out, were best friends and had been for years. The pitcher knew even before he released that final pitch that victory was on the line, but so was the pain of failure. He fully expected to win, but he wouldn't celebrate victory until he had consoled the friend he had defeated.

Few of us—okay, almost none of us—display that type of empathy when we win, but all of us—every one of us—has experienced the pain of failure. Author J. K. Rowling famously pointed out that, "It is impossible to live without failing at something, unless you live so cautiously that you might as well not have lived at all—in which case, you fail by default."[1]

Whether she knew it or not, Rowling was putting her spin on a biblical truth: failure is inevitable.

So, how do we endure failure, learn from it, and make the most of it?

First of all, we need to understand it better. Failure is simply the result of an inadequate measurement against some kind of standard. So, it may or may not be sin. The batter failed when he struck out to end the game, but striking out wasn't a sin. Likewise, some of our failures are sin and some are not.

We fail for all sorts of reasons—poor planning, unexpected circumstances, lack of skill, the skill (or malice) of others. We also have different types of failures—task failures, work or career failures, relational failures, moral failures. And we react to failure in all sorts of ways, typically with emotions like shame, fear, confusion, disgrace, doubt, loneliness, denial, and anger.

We generally want there to be a villain or some other cause we can blame for our failures. Sometimes, however, there is no one or nothing to blame. Ask Job, the Old Testament saint with a book about his life. Some failures are simply part of the larger drama, and we won't get a reason or fully understand the lesson on this side of heaven. At the same time, we're only hurting ourselves—and failing further—when we shirk responsibility, lash out at others, rationalize mistakes, or otherwise deny ownership of our failures.

Satan wants us to either internalize our failure ("I am a failure") or externalize our failure ("Everyone has failed me"). But there's another choice: we can surrender our failure.

Here's the gospel in four words: People fail. God rescues.

Surrendering our failure begins with owning it. People tend to understand that idea intellectually but practice it poorly. Most of us work like crazy to present an image that doesn't include failure. We defend it, deny it, justify it, reassign it, or cover it up. But 1 John 1:8–10 says we are "deceiving ourselves" and we are a "liar" if we think we have no sin. If we confess our sin, on the other hand, it says God is faithful to forgive us. And Proverbs 28:13 says, "The one who conceals his sins will not prosper, but whoever confesses and renounces them will find mercy."

Surrendering our failures also involves holding to God's promises. We often don't get the answers, but that's why faith is so important when navigating the challenges of life.

Job didn't get the answers to his questions about his suffering, but he wrapped his heart and soul around his personal core beliefs, one of which was that God is good and fair. He clung to that truth.

When God allows us to experience failure that's no fault of our own, we also can cling to that truth. When we cause our own failure, from sin or for some other reason, we can remember the truth of the gospel: People fail. God rescues.

Nobody seeks to fail or plans to fail, but failure eventually finds us all. Our failures won't define us, but how we respond to them very likely will. Failures can become open wounds that never heal, or scars of honor that tell the stories of lessons learned by clinging to God when it has mattered most.

Insights to Deposit

1. Face failure for what it is . . . or isn't.

2. We often are called to ride through a failure with a friend. Learn to practice empathy.

3. Failure isn't fatal. Proverbs 24:16 says, "Though a righteous person falls seven times, he will get up, but the wicked will stumble into ruin." Oswald Chambers put it this way: "Trust God and do the next thing."[2]

4. Hold to God's promises.

Questions

1. What is the first significant failure you remember experiencing in life?

2. How do you generally react to failures that are clearly of your own making? What about your failures that are clearly caused by others?

3. What does it look like to practice empathy when walking through a failure with a friend?

4. What are some lessons you've learned from failing?

Digesting Success

*Most people handle failure
far better than success.*

I f you think failure is challenging, you should try the alternative.

That probably sounds strange. A little counterintuitive. After all, everyone wants to win—to succeed in sports, in work, in relationships, in all of life. And, yet, feasting on a steady diet of success is a sure path to indigestion.

In fact, I've become convinced that most people handle failure far better than success. I've seen it in the lives of the business leaders with whom I've worked. I've seen it in politicians, in athletes, in actors, and other celebrities who regularly make the news. And I've seen it in the stories of average folks who win the lottery.

Who doesn't want to win the lottery, right? Well, research continues to show that lottery winners are more likely to declare bankruptcy within three to five years than the average American, and that winning the lottery won't make you happier or healthier than anyone else in the world.

Perhaps that's why Albert Einstein once said, "Try not to become a man of success, but rather try to become a man of value."[1] It's also why my conversations with Kile not only included discussions about defining success and enduring failure, but also about digesting success.

When you digest something, you've broken it down and it becomes part of the body, not just an attachment on the side or something that sticks in your gut and causes pain. Success is something you fully consume, or else it will fully consume you. That's because success, if left undigested, feeds the monster of pride.

With success come the trappings of success—congratulatory praises for the star athlete from well-meaning friends, family, and fans; a bigger office, a fancy title, a higher salary, and other perks for the rising-star executive; standing ovations for the speaker or preacher; honors and accolades for the straight-A student.

With success comes a sense of entitlement. People simply treat you differently when you're successful. They don't question your decisions as often or as forcefully. They go to greater lengths to accommodate your whims. They ask your opinion, even if you have no particular expertise on a subject. And they laugh at your jokes, even if they aren't funny.

It all seems great until you wake up and realize success is costing you everything that really matters because you've slowly abandoned the beliefs and the people who got you to the top.

Proverbs 27:21 says, "A crucible refines silver, a smelter refines gold, and a person refines his praise."

I'm not anti-success, mind you. I've just seen what it can do to good people who have digested it poorly. I've coached and watched people who have learned the real-world truth of

Matthew 16:26: "For what will it benefit someone if he gains the whole world yet loses his life? Or what will anyone give in exchange for his life?"

On the other hand, I've also seen the undeniable good people can do with success when they digest it properly. When they use their authority, their finances, and their acclaim to help others and to serve God, they always end up living a more fulfilled, satisfied life.

Digesting success is a simple but challenging matter of remembering—remembering who helped you in your success, remembering the more noble purposes of success, and, most of all, remembering the deepest source of success: God.

Read Deuteronomy 8, especially verses 17–19: "You may say to yourself, 'My power and my own ability have gained this wealth for me,' but remember that the LORD your God gives you the power to gain wealth, in order to confirm his covenant he swore to your fathers, as it is today. If you ever forget the LORD your God and follow other gods to serve them and bow in worship to them, I testify against you today that you will perish."

Success easily becomes an idol, a false god we serve. And that will always leave us spiritually sick.

Insights to Deposit

1. Success, understood rightly, should increase your humility and rein in your arrogance.

2. Success should cause you to think, "Look what God enabled me to do!" instead of "Look what I've done."

3. Opening your mind and heart to frank feedback from God's Word, the Holy Spirit, and godly advisors helps you properly digest success.

Questions

1. Think about the lives of Joseph, Solomon, David, and Jesus. How did they handle or fail to handle success?

2. A. W. Tozer said, "Complacency is a deadly foe of all spiritual growth."[2] How does that comment relate to digesting success?

3. What are some of your experiences with success, either how you've handled personal success or how you've witnessed others handle it?

Having Fun

Fun is not the primary goal of life,
but it sure helps us enjoy the journey.

Abraham Maslow began his life just like the rest of us—as a baby who grew into a child. Then things got a bit more interesting.

Maslow was born in 1908, the oldest of seven children born to Jewish immigrants from Kiev. The family lived in a multicultural neighborhood in Brooklyn, New York, where young Abraham was regularly harassed by anti-Semites. His parents were poor and uneducated, he had very few friends as a child, his father was absent for long stretches, and he came to despise his mother.

The future didn't look great for Maslow. But he spent much of his childhood in libraries, went to college, became a professor, and now is best known for coming up with a famous model that illustrates human beings' "hierarchy of needs."

You might be surprised, given Maslow's dysfunctional beginnings and highly academic career, that the photo of Maslow on his Wikipedia page shows a man who is smiling and looks very happy. I can't confirm it, but my guess is that hard work and intellectual pursuits weren't the only reasons Maslow overcame considerable odds and had an influential life. I suspect there was another factor in the equation—fun.

The pyramid graphic of Maslow's hierarchy of needs doesn't mention fun, but I can't imagine life without it. Malow's theory was pretty simple: There is an order—a hierarchy—for the way humans pursue our needs. First, we pursue our basic physiological needs, such as food, water, warmth, and rest. Then we go for safety and security needs. Only when those are met do we move toward psychological needs—intimate relationships and friendship, then needs related to esteem, such as prestige or feelings of accomplishment. If those are met, we advance to the ultimate need of self-fulfillment through self-actualization—achieving our full potential, including creative activities.

If I were to plug fun into that model, it wouldn't be at the top of the pyramid, but near the base. If you've ever travelled to a third-world country where poverty is real, you surely noticed that kids there still pursued fun. It's like a basic instinct. They might need food and water for survival, but kids around the world often put fun ahead of safety. I've never been around a kid, no matter how desperate his or her living conditions, who passed up the opportunity to have some fun.

In America, we tend to equate fun with leisure and play. They aren't the same things, although they certainly are close relatives. Play often is fun, but sometimes it is hard work and at other times it's no fun at all. Leisure is usually fun, but fun doesn't have to come from leisure. As I pointed out, kids in developing countries gravitate toward fun, but they seldom experience leisure.

I love to fish (you may have caught on to that fact by now). I have great fun on fishing trips with my good friends, especially when we fly to some remote location and camp on a river for a few days. That's fun. And leisure. But fun doesn't have to be exotic or expensive. I have fun fishing in the rivers and lakes near my home, riding my bike, or watering the trees in my yard (even when they don't need it). And I have fun at work.

Dr. Seuss, who wrote more than sixty books that have sold more than six hundred million copies, put it this way: "It is fun to have fun."[1]

It's also *important* to have fun. There is a train of thought that says if you are going to be a fervent Christian you can never laugh, smile, and have fun. To be holy, goes this line of thinking, is to be serious all the time. That is just not true. When Zechariah described a revitalized Jerusalem, his prophesy said, "The streets of the city will be filled with boys and girls playing in them" (Zech. 8:5). And one of Solomon's conclusions about life was that, "There is nothing better for a person than to eat, drink, and enjoy his work. I have seen that even this is from God's hand" (Eccl. 2:24).

Hedonists rush headlong to an extreme that says life is all about fun—all about our personal pleasure, self-indulgence, and happiness. They've taken God out of the equation. Ascetics rush to the other end of the spectrum—life, they say, is all about self-denial. Maturity, meanwhile, requires us to take seriously the things of life that are serious, including our faith. It requires sacrifice, hard work, and a focus on the tasks at hand, many of which are not fun. But we can't take fun out of the equation. It's not the primary goal of life, but it sure helps us enjoy the journey.

God created us to have fun—not *instead of worshiping* Him, but *as we worship Him*. The apostle Paul put it this way: "So, whether you eat or drink, or whatever you do, do everything for the glory of God" (1 Cor. 10:31). That word *whatever* means . . . well, *whatever*. So, it includes things that are fun.

Insights to Deposit

1. Don't feel guilty or shallow because you are having fun. ("People rarely succeed unless they have fun in what they are doing."[2] —Dale Carnegie)

2. The ability to play well with others is one of the first social expressions we look for in human development, and it remains a vital quality in the most edifying relationships. ("You can discover more about a person in an hour of play than in a year of conversation." —Plato)

3. Fun sparks creativity and innovation. ("Play is the answer to the question, 'How does anything new come about?'"[3] —Jean Piaget)

4. By-products of fun include hopefulness and gratitude. ("You just have to decide whether you're a Tigger or an Eeyore."[4] —Randy Pausch)

Questions

1. What role does your ability to have fun play in sharing the gospel?

2. How does fun affect your attitude?

3. What dangers are there in comparing how much fun you have in life with what you see in the lives of others—either those who seem to do nothing but have fun or those who seem never to have fun?

4. How have you found opportunities to bring fun into your school/church/work/relationships?

Finishing Well

It is never too soon to imagine the
ending of your life and work.

The five longest NCAA football games on record all went to seven overtimes, and two of them involved the Arkansas Razorbacks.

The University of Arkansas is in Fayetteville, Arkansas, which is where we've made our home for more than thirty years. So, I vividly remember both games, but especially the win for Arkansas over Ole Miss. Previously, no game had gone more than four overtime periods, so it didn't take long before it etched a spot in the history books. Both teams were exhausted and seemed to be hanging on by a thread as they battled back and forth for more than four hours. I was exhausted, and I had been sitting on my cushy couch inside my air-conditioned house the entire afternoon.

In the end, both teams made it to the last play—an incomplete pass from Eli Manning on a two-point conversion attempt that left Arkansas with the 58–56 victory.

Sure, I celebrated because the team I pulled for won the game. But I took something else away from that game—something that I got from watching both teams play hard to the last whistle.

As the game progressed from overtime to overtime, neither team said, "We forfeit—y'all can just have this one." Neither team said, "Hey, we have some parties to get to and it's getting late. We're pretty tired, so we'll see you next time."

No way! Both teams had invested hours and hours of practice. They had sacrificed time and energy, worked through pain, and wanted the payoff that comes with victory. They were driven by a clear goal and were intent on finishing well, regardless of how long it took to finish the game.

Life is often like a seven-overtime football game—a long, grueling test that's full of highs and lows. We can score touchdowns that make us think we've got it won, so we begin to slack off. And we can miss a tackle that makes us think we've lost and there's no hope. But after every play, good or bad, we need to get up and give the next play our best effort and finish well.

How do we do this?

First, we define the real finish line.

There are short-term, mid-term, and long-term goals we need to accomplish throughout life. Many of them are important, and, generally speaking, it's good to finish what we start. If you are mowing the grass and see a child wandering alone toward a busy highway, however, you don't add, "help child" to the end of your to-do list and get back to your lawn. You stop your yard work and take care of the child!

That's an extreme example, but I see this in life all the time, especially in business; people become so focused on a goal that they fail to pivot based on new information or new circumstances.

In most of life, we can ditch the end goal and adjust when the situation calls for it. But there is one ending that can't be changed. Death is certain. And the sooner we can fix our aspirations around finishing that race well, the better. Other starts and finishes along the way are still important, but they all roll into this final finish line.

For men of faith, finishing well is about pleasing God with our lives—it's consistently loving God and loving others, not just at the beginning but all the way to the end, and then hearing the words *Well done* from Jesus. I think this is what Paul is talking about in 2 Timothy 4:7 when he says he "fought the good fight" during his life. He didn't get lost or sidetracked by bad fights; he had Jesus as his finish line. And having Jesus as the finish line shapes all the other races we run along the way.

Second, we suspend our disbelief.

In 2 Timothy 4:7–8, Paul not only says he fought the good fight, but that he "kept the faith." We can't finish well on our own power, but only by the grace of God—and that requires faith, especially when life gets tough.

Hebrews 11:8–10 tells us about Abraham's great faith. By faith, Abraham lived a transient life for years because he trusted God with his future and because he believed in an ultimate vision and goal for his life—eternal life with the Creator God, "For he was looking forward to the city that has foundations, whose architect and builder is God" (Heb. 11:10).

Abraham made plenty of mistakes along the way, but Romans 4 tells us he didn't waver "in unbelief" and was "strengthened in his faith." He finished well, and his faith was "credited to him for righteousness" (Rom. 4:20–22).

We may not always be able to see the road ahead clearly, much less the finish line and what lies beyond it. But by faith, we know it's there, and that God will carry us through.

Third, we take a long view of life.

The inscription on the grave of Ruth Bell Graham was inspired by a sign she once saw on a highway. It reads, "End of Construction. Thank you for your patience." The wife of the late, great evangelist Billy Graham knew that we're all a work in progress and, as Eugene Peterson put it in his classic book, that life requires a "long obedience in the same direction."[1]

Finishing well involves patience and perseverance, which both come with a long view of life. Galatians 6:9 tells us not to "get tired of doing good, for we will reap at the proper time if we don't give up." And Philippians 1:6 says, "I am sure of this, that he who started a good work in you will carry it on to completion until the day of Christ Jesus."

With the long view, we understand that life doesn't end when something bad happens. As Mike Ditka put it, "Success isn't permanent, and failure isn't fatal."[2]

With the long view, we understand that success doesn't release us from the need to grow. A long view keeps us humble in success, realizing that our temporal gains, though sweet and worthy of celebration, are merely a drop in the bucket of life.

With the long view, we understand everything isn't bound by our immediate circumstances. We can relax and become more accepting. Small slights and inconveniences carry less weight, forgiveness comes more easily, and we're less likely to end up bitter old men.

Insights to Deposit

1. Identify the enemies of your strong finish. ("Therefore, since we also have such a large cloud of witnesses surrounding us, let us lay aside every hindrance and the sin that so easily ensnares us. Let us run with endurance the race that lies before us." —Heb. 12:1)

2. Strive for consistency. Some men have trouble getting started. Don't be that guy. Some men are strong out of the gate, but they don't have the qualities to endure and finish well. Don't be that guy. ("Starting strong is good. Finishing strong is epic."[3] —author Robin Sharma)

3. Leave a godly legacy. ("The most important part of a story is the ending. No one reads a book to get to the middle."[4] —crime novelist Mickey Spillane)

Questions

1. How would you define and describe the ultimate finish line for your life? In other words, what does *finishing well* look like for you personally? What would you want on your tombstone?

2. Write an obituary for yourself. What would you want it to say? How would you want people to remember you? Begin practicing for that now.

3. What are some things that motivate you to finish well?

4. What are some things that cause you to struggle with consistency toward long-term goals?

Conclusion

Nor deem the irrevocable Past,
As wholly wasted, wholly vain,
If, rising on its wrecks, at last
To something nobler we attain.[1]

—Henry Wadsworth Longfellow

When Kile graduated from high school, we celebrated the occasion much like anyone else. Family and friends came in for the event. We took lots of photos of him in his purple cap and gown. We lifted our glasses to toast his accomplishments. And because major milestones require some token of appreciation, we gave him a few gifts to express our gratitude for his hard work and to help launch him into the next phase of his life.

One of those gifts, of course, was that leather-bound journal purchased a few years earlier at a small shop in Italy that now included the handwritten notes from our discussions about the forty-one deposits you've found in this book. It was wrapped and included a note that expressed my enduring love for him.

And what about the other nine deposits that were on my original list? Well, they were sort of like the walk-on player on a great college basketball team—they were important, but they just didn't get into this particular game. We've discussed some of them since Kile graduated from high school, but not using this format. I didn't hold onto the journal until it was "finished," because that was never the point.

The point, as you recall, was to invest some life-lessons as deposits into my son as a way of strengthening our heart-knot. And while we might have left a few deposits on the bench when the final buzzer sounded, that bigger goal of strengthening that knot was achieved.

I can't say for sure how much of the specific content from our discussions Kile remembers or leans into regularly, but his adult life is off to a wonderful start and our relationship continues to grow. Kile not only graduated high school, but went on to college, graduated, earned a spot in a prestigious leadership program with a Fortune 100 company, joined some buddies to start a new company, and, most recently, married the love of his life. His life isn't perfect and he makes mistakes—after all, he is his father's son—but I am bursting with pride at the man he has become.

And, by the way, I also benefited from our discussions, perhaps even more than Kile. I benefit from the personal study I put into it. I benefited from the thought-provoking questions he asked. The topics drove me back to a desperate place with my Creator. And finally, the conversations helped propel my learning how to parent three adult children.

Kile and I still meet for a bagel once every now and then, but the discussions are even less structured. Like his sisters, he's an adult who owns his faith and makes his own decisions. Our relationship has shifted. I'm learning to be respectful of his independence, while happily serving as a sounding board or advisor when those opportunities arise.

Mostly, I'm just happy that he enjoys spending time with me, because I love spending time with him. That's a sweet fruit of parenting. Our children grow up and move on, sometimes to other cities, but they never leave our hearts. If we've made some good deposits and continue to strengthen the heart-knot, the nest might empty, but the relationship only grows stronger.

That's my hope and prayer for everyone who reads and uses this book—that you will strengthen the heart-knot with your child for the phase of life you're in and for every phase of life to come. It may not be easy. In fact, it will most likely be hard. But you will never regret it.

Notes

Introduction: Heart-Knot Deposits

1. "About one-third of U.S. children are living with an unmarried parent," by Gretchen Livingston, Pew Research Center, April 27, 2018.
2. "The Father Absence Crisis," by Melissa Steward, the National Fatherhood Initiative, February 16, 2017.

Part 1: My Faith

1. MLK Quote of the Week: The King Center, Feb. 21, 2013, http://www.thekingcenter.org/blog/mlk-quote-week-faith-taking-first-step.

Fearing God

1. "Whatever Happened to the Fear of God?" by John MacArthur, Grace to You, August 10, 2016, https://www.gty.org/library/blog/B160810/whatever-happened-to-the-fear-of-god.
2. "The man who fears God has nothing else to fear, he is guarded in his conscious and unconscious life, in his waking and his sleeping moments." Oswald Chambers, *Shade of His Hand: Talks on the Book of Ecclesiastes* (Grand Rapids, MI: Discovery House, 2015).
3. Oswald Chambers, *The Highest Good—The Pilgrim's Song Book* (Grand Rapids, MI: Discovery House, 1965), Psalm 128.

Hearing God

1. Henry T. Blackaby and Richard Blackaby, *Hearing God's Voice* (Nashville: B&H Publishing Group, 2002), 18.

2. Rick Warren sermon titled "Don't Give Up, Look Up—Part 2" (2018). Accessed at https://pastorrick.com/player/?bid=da9bfaa6 -9b5f-41a0-a33b-bffc7eab93c9. Also posted on his Twitter account Feb. 26, 2015, https://twitter.com/RickWarren/status /571010599422812161.

3. Dallas Willard, *Hearing God: Developing a Conversational Relationship with God* (Downers Grove, IL: InterVarsity Press, 2012).

Resisting Temptation

1. Ralph Waldo Emerson, *Essays: First Series*, 1847 edition.

2. "Sin Will Never Make You Happy, by John Piper," Desiring God, November 26, 2016, https://www.desiringgod.org/articles /sin-will-never-make-you-happy.

Worshiping God

1. Martin Luther in *Luther's Large Catechism: God's Call to Repentance, Faith and Prayer*, trans. John Nicholas Lenker (Minneapolis: Luther Press, 1908), 44.

2. James K. A. Smith, *You Are What You Love: The Spiritual Power of Habit* (Grand Rapids, MI: Brazos Press, 2016), 10.

3. A. W. Tozer, *The Knowledge of the Holy* (New York: HarperCollins, 1961), 1.

4. Timothy Keller, *Counterfeit Gods: The Empty Promises of Money, Sex, and Power, and the Only Hope That Matters* (New York: Penguin, 2009), xx.

5. Ibid.

6. Rick Warren, *The Purpose Driven Life: What on Earth Am I Here For?* (Grand Rapids, MI: Zondervan, 2002), 84.

7. Sinclair B. Ferguson, *A Heart for God* (Carlisle, PA: Banner of Truth Trust, 1987), 111–12.

Taking Responsiblity

1. If you want to see a video of the falling satellite, go to YouTube and search "When Satellite Dishes Fall from the Sky." It should be the first result.

2. "Quotable" Quotes by the editors of *Reader's Digest*, March 31, 1997 (attributes the quote to *Fortune*).

3. *Spider-Man*, directed by Sam Rami (Marvel Enterprises; Laura Zisken Productions: 2002).

4. P. J. O'Rourke, *Rolling Stone* (November 30, 1989).

5. Robertson McQuilkin, "Living by Vows," *Christianity Today*, February 1, 2004.

Asking Questions

1. As quoted in "How to Consult Like Peter Drucker," by Rick Wartzman, *Forbes*, Sept. 11, 2012, https://www.forbes.com/sites/drucker/2012/09/11/how-to-consult-like-peter-drucker/#ba09d572e49e. Note: Wartzman is Director of the KH Moon Center for a Functioning Society at the Drucker Institute and served as the organization's executive director from its founding in 2007 until early 2016.

2. Twitter, accessed September 27, 2012, https://twitter.com/simonsinek/status/251423130927644672.

3. Statement to William Miller, as quoted in *LIFE* magazine (May 2, 1955) and in Joseph S. Willis, *Finding Faith in the Face of Doubt: A Guide for Contemporary Seekers* (Wheaton, IL: Quest Books, 2001), 58.

Talking Straight

1. Notebook entry, January or February 1894, *Mark Twain's Notebook*, ed. Albert Bigelow Paine (New York: Harper & Brothers, 1935), 240.

Staying Pure

1. C. S. Lewis, *Mere Christianity* (1952; repr., New York: HarperCollins, 2001), 95.

Living Daily

1. Brother Lawrence, *The Practice of the Presence of God* (1673; repr., Peabody, MA: Hendrickson Publishers, 2011), 52.

2. Francis Schaeffer, *True Spirituality* (1971; repr., Wheaton, IL: Tyndale, 2001), 8.

3. Martin Luther King Jr., sermon "The Three Dimensions of a Complete Life," delivered at New Covenant Baptist Church in Chicago, April 9, 1967; see https://kinginstitute.stanford.edu/.

Embracing Manhood

1. "John Eldredge Speaks on Ransoming Hearts," by Laura Bagby, CBN Spiritual Life, undated, www1.cbn.com/biblestudy /john-eldredge-speaks-on-ransoming-hearts, accessed December 11, 2018.

Fighting Perfectionism

1. Stephen Manes, *Be a Perfect Person in Just Three Days!* (New York: Random House, 1998), 72.

Developing Perseverance

1. William Shakespeare, *Henry VI*, Part III, Act II, scene 1, line 54.

2. Mary Anne Radmacher, *Courage Doesn't Always Roar* (Newburyport, MA: Conari Press, 2009).

3. C. S. Lewis, *Mere Christianity* (1952; repr., New York: HarperOne, 2001), 28.

4. Walter Elliott, *The Spiritual Life: Doctrine and Practice of Christian Perfection* (New York: The Paulist Press, 1918), 364.

5. R. C. Sproul, *Classic Teachings on the Nature of God* (Peabody, MA: Hendrickson, 2010), 254.

6. William Penn, *Some Fruits of Solitude in Reflections & Maxims* (New York: Scott-Thaw Company, 1693), 13.

Part 3: My Heart

1. Martin Luther in *Luther's Large Catechism: God's Call to Repentance, Faith and Prayer*, trans. John Nicholas Lenker (Minneapolis: Luther Press, 1908), 44.

Learning Contentment

1. C. S. Lewis, *Mere Christianity* (1952; repr., New York: HarperCollins, 2001), 213.

Practicing Rest

1. "The troubling case of the young Japanese reporter who worked herself to death," by Eli Rosenberg, *Washington Post*, October 5, 2017. https://www.washingtonpost.com/news/world-views/wp/2017/10/05/the-troubling-case-of-the-young-japanese-reporter-who-worked-herself-to-death/?utm_term=.f72385663f69 (accessed June 27, 2018).

2. https://hbr.org/2018/07/the-leaders-calendar#how-ceos-manage-time

3. Walter Brueggemann, *Journey to the Common Good* (Louisville, KY: Westminster John Knox Press, 2010).

4. Andy Crouch, *Playing God: Redeeming the Gift of Power* (Downers Grove, IL: InterVarsity Press, 2013), 117.

Chasing Balance

1. Simon Sinek, "Sacrifice Should Be Worth the Sacrifice," https://blog.startwithwhy.com/refocus/2011/02/sacrifice-should-be-worth-the-sacrifice.html.

2. This is from Dave Ramsey's Financial Peace University video, Lesson 3: Cash Flow Planning (about 34 minutes in).

3. http://www.quotationspage.com/quote/26495.html

Reflecting Joy

1. You can learn more at https://whatsinside.it/#!/lincolnmarkham.

2. C. S. Lewis, *The Business of Heaven: Daily Readings* (New York: HarperCollins, 2017), quoting from *Letters to Malcolm*, chap. 17.

3. John Piper, "How Do You Define Joy?," Desiring God, July 25, 2015, https://www.desiringgod.org/articles/how-do-you-define-joy.

4. Il'ia L'ovovich Tolstoy, *Reminiscences of Tolstoy* (New York: Century Company, 1914), 324.

Finding Peace

1. Mark Saviers, with Robyn and Tommy Van Zandt, *Flipped: How One Man's Tragic Fall Became a Story of Surrender, Faith, and Hope* (Colorado Springs: Book Villages, 2018).

Part 4: My Relationships

1. Timothy J. Keller, *The Reason for God: Belief in an Age of Skepticism* (New York: Penguin, 2008), 10.

Loving People

1. Author conversation with Louie Giglio.

2. Mark Twain, *Bite-Size Twain: Wit and Wisdom from the Literary Legend* (New York: St. Martin's Press, 2015).

Standing Alone

1. https://theodoreroosevelt.com/theodore-roosevelt-quotes/

Getting Married

1. Full quote is "Men, you'll never be a good groom to your wife unless you're first a good bride to Jesus." From a sermon, "Love, Lust, and Liberation" by Timothy J. Keller, April 25, 1999, https://gospelinlife.com/downloads/love-lust-and-liberation-5087/.

2. Timothy and Kathy Keller, *The Meaning of Marriage: Facing the Complexities of Commitment with the Wisdom of God* (New York: Penguin Publishing Group, 2013), 83.

Building Family

1. For the record, none of us have ever had tea with the queen.

Part 5: My Work

1. Abraham Maslow, *Motivation and Personality* (New York: Harper & Row, 1970), 46.

Setting Goals

1. Yogi Berra, quoted in Dave Kaplan, *When You Come to a Fork in the Road, Take It!: Inspiration and Wisdom from One of Baseball's Greatest Heroes* (New York: Hyperion, 2001), 53.

2. Brian Tracy, *Eat That Frog! 21 Great Ways to Stop Procrastinating and Get More Done in Less Time* (Oakland, CA: Berrett-Koehler Publishers, 2017), 10.

Working Hard

1. George Herman ("Babe") Ruth, "Bat It Out!" in *The Rotarian* (July 14, 1940), 12–14.

2. Oren Harari, *The Leadership Secrets of Colin Powell* (New York: McGraw-Hill, 2003), 164.

Handling Money

1. Letter from Thomas Jefferson to his granddaughter, Cornelia Jefferson Randolph, "A Decalogue of Canons for Observation in Practical Life" (1825).

2. John L. Mason, *An Enemy Called Average* (Tulsa, OK: Insight International, 1990), 55.

3. Dave Ramsey, *The Total Money Makeover: A Proven Plan for Financial Fitness* (Nashville, TN: Thomas Nelson, 2013), 29.

4. In the essay "Of Seditions and Troubles," which can be found in multiple collections, including Francis Bacon, *The Essays* (UK: Penguin, 1985).

5. https://www.brainyquote.com/quotes/gary_vaynerchuk_503163

Finding Your Calling

1. Stephen Caldwell, "Finding Your Job Fit," *Life@Work* Volume 1, Number 3, August 1998

2. Ibid.

3. From *The Babylonian Captivity of the Church*, 1520, as found in Paul W. Robinson, *The Annotated Luther, Volume 3: Church and Sacraments* (Minneapolis, MN: Fortress Press, 2016).

Part 6: My Future

1. Tony Evans, Twitter, June 30, 2018.

Defining Success

1. Erwin W. Lutzer, *Failure: The Back Door to Success* (Chicago, IL: Moody, 2016), 155.

2. *The Westminster Collection of Christian Quotations*, ed. Martin H. Manser (Louisville, KY: Westminster John Knox Press, 2001).

Thinking Ahead

1. The trend stats are widely quoted (e.g., "Why many teens don't want to get a driver's license," PBS, March 6, 2017, or "Teen Driving by the Numbers," *Wired*, March 27, 2018, www.wired.com/story/teen-driving-numbers/). They originate from http://www.monitoringthefuture.org/. The non-stat stuff mostly came from "Have Smartphones Destroyed a Generation?" by Jean Twenge, *The Atlantic*, Aug. 3, 2017.

Making Decisions

1. As quoted in several books, including John C. Maxwell, *Beyond Talent: Become Someone Who Gets Extraordinary Results* (Nashville, TN: Thomas Nelson, 2011). (Maxwell includes this as the second sentence: "They seldom win the solid respect of their fellows.") The saying is also attributed as a Chinese Proverb, according to Dr. Raghu Korrapati, *108 Pearls of Wisdom: For Every College Student* (Diamond Pocket Books Pvt Ltd, 2015), but it doesn't come across as a Chinese proverb to me.

2. As quoted in numerous books, including by John Maxwell in *The 360 Degree Leader: Developing Your Influence from Anywhere in the Organization*, by John Maxwell (Nashville, TN: Thomas Nelson Inc., 2006). There are several variants of this quote in other sources, most notably *Think Out of the Box* by Mike Vance and Diane Deacon (n.p.: Carter Press, 1995).

Enduring Failure

1. Harvard University Commencement Address (June 5, 2008), https://vimeo.com/1711302.

2. David McCasland, *Oswald Chambers: Abandoned to God: The Life Story of the Author of My Utmost for His Highest* (Grand Rapids, MI: Discovery House Publishers, 1993), 177.

Digesting Success

1. As quoted by *LIFE* magazine (May 2, 1955).

2. A. W. Tozer, *The Pursuit of God* (Shawnee, KS: Gideon House Books, 2017). Interestingly, he also wrote (in *The Size of the Soul*) that "Complacency is the deadly enemy of spiritual progress. The contented soul is the stagnant soul."

Having Fun

1. Dr. Seuss, *The Cat in the Hat* (1957; repr., New York: Random House Children's Books, 2012), 18.

2. Quoted in Jill Murphy Long, *Permission to Play: Taking Time to Renew Your Smile* (Naperville, IL: Sourcebooks, Inc., 2003), 69.

3. Quoted in *American Journal of Play, Volume 1* (University of Illinois Press, 2008).

4. Quoted in Mark Strassmann, "Randy Pausch's 'Last Lecture' Legacy," CBS (September 13, 2010), https://www.cbsnews.com/news/randy-pauschs-last-lecture-legacy/.

Finishing Well

1. Eugene H. Peterson, *A Long Obedience in the Same Direction: Discipleship in an Instant Society* by (Downers Grove, IL: IVP Books; 20th Anniversary edition, 2000).

2. "Success isn't permanent, and failure isn't fatal." —Mike Ditka, according to quoteinvestigator.com . . . 990, *The Fourth—and by Far the Most Recent—637 Best Things Anybody Ever Said* by Robert Byrne.

3. Twitter; accessed November 14 2013, https://twitter.com/robinsharma/status/400981431976873986?lang=en.

4. *Quotable Quotes: Wit and Wisdom from the Greatest Minds of Our Time*, by the editors of *Reader's Digest* (White Plains, NY: Reader's Digest, 2013), 157.

Conclusion

1. Henry Wadsworth Longfellow, "The Ladder of Saint Augustine."

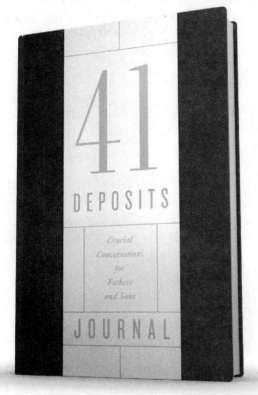